**"What's making you tired
is the amount of work
you do NOT do.**

"Remember the day last week when you were
constantly interrupted? No letters answered.
Appointments broken. Trouble here and there.
Everything went wrong that day. You accomplished nothing, yet you went home exhausted
—with a splitting headache.

"The next day everything clicked at the office.
You accomplished forty times more than you
did the previous day. Yet you went home
fresh as a snowy-white gardenia. You have
had that experience. So have I.

"The lesson to be learned? Just this: our fatigue is often caused not by work, but by
worry, frustration, and resentment."

—Dale Carnegie

Books by Dale Carnegie

How to Develop Self-Confidence and Influence
    People by Public Speaking
How to Enjoy Your Life and Your Job
How to Stop Worrying and Start Living
How to Win Friends and Influence People
The Quick and Easy Way to
    Effective Speaking

Published by POCKET BOOKS

How To Enjoy Your Life and Your Job

Selections from *How to Win Friends and Influence People* and *How to Stop Worrying and Start Living*

by Dale Carnegie

Foreword by Dorothy Carnegie
PRESIDENT, DALE CARNEGIE AND ASSOCIATES, INC.

PUBLISHED BY POCKET BOOKS NEW YORK

POCKET BOOKS, a Simon & Schuster division of
GULF & WESTERN CORPORATION
1230 Avenue of the Americas, New York, N.Y. 10020

Published by arrangement with Simon and Schuster
Library of Congress Catalog Card Number: 73-132774

ISBN: 0-671-41761-4

First Pocket Books printing May, 1974

15   14   13   12

POCKET and colophon are trademarks of Simon & Schuster.

Printed in the U.S.A.

Contents

EXCERPTS FROM *HOW TO STOP WORRYING AND START LIVING*

Part One

SEVEN WAYS TO PEACE AND HAPPINESS

EXCERPTS FROM *HOW TO WIN FRIENDS
AND INFLUENCE PEOPLE*

Part Two

FUNDAMENTAL TECHNIQUES
IN HANDLING PEOPLE

Part Three

WAYS TO WIN PEOPLE
TO YOUR WAY OF THINKING

Part Four

WAYS TO CHANGE PEOPLE
WITHOUT GIVING OFFENSE
OR AROUSING RESENTMENT

Foreword

BY DOROTHY CARNEGIE

Did you ever stop to think that most of us spend the greater part of our lives on the job—whatever that job may be?

This means that our attitude towards our job can determine whether our days are filled with excitement and the sense of fulfillment that comes from top performance —or with frustration, boredom and fatigue.

Dale Carnegie training is designed to help you get the most out of your working day in terms of job-satisfaction by getting the most out of yourself all the time. As you study these pages, evaluate your own approach to life and people. Then start to build on your strengths and discover how many talents and abilities you actually have that you didn't even know you had—and how much fun it is to use these abilities.

This book is a collection of chapters selected from Dale Carnegie's two best sellers, How to Win Friends and Influence People and How to Stop Worrying and Start Living. We have selected those portions of each book most relevant to people like yourself who are enrolled in a Dale Carnegie course. You want more fulfillment in your life, a sense of harmony and purpose, a feeling that you're making the best use of your inner resources—and this book will help you achieve these aims.

Participation in Dale Carnegie training is an adventure in self-discovery; and it could be a turning point in your life. You already possess hidden assets within yourself

*that can make your life glorious. All you need now is
the determination to uncover and use them.*

DOROTHY CARNEGIE, PRESIDENT
DALE CARNEGIE & ASSOCIATES, INC.

Part One

Seven Ways
to Peace
and
Happiness

Dale Carnegie wrote his book *How to Stop Worrying and Start Living* to show that life is very much what we make it. If we first learn to accept ourselves, seeing the good as clearly as the not-so-good, and then get busy doing the things necessary to reach our goals, we will be less likely to have either the need or the inclination to lose time and energy worrying.

Chapter 1

FIND YOURSELF AND BE YOURSELF:
REMEMBER THERE IS NO ONE
ELSE ON EARTH LIKE YOU

I have a letter from Mrs. Edith Allred, of Mount Airy, North Carolina: "As a child, I was extremely sensitive and shy," she says in her letter. "I was always overweight and my cheeks made me look even fatter than I was. I had an old-fashioned mother who thought it was foolish to make clothes look pretty. She always said: 'Wide will wear while narrow will tear'; and she dressed me accordingly. I never went to parties; never had any fun; and when I went to school, I never joined the other children in outside activities, not even athletics. I was morbidly shy. I felt I was 'different' from everybody else, and entirely undesirable.

"When I grew up, I married a man who was several years my senior. But I didn't change. My in-laws were a poised and self-confident family. They were everything I should have been but simply was not. I tried my best to be like them, but I couldn't. Every attempt they made to draw me out of myself only drove me further into my shell. I became nervous and irritable. I avoided all friends. I got so bad I even dreaded the sound of the doorbell ringing! I was a failure. I knew it; and I was afraid my husband would find it out. So, whenever we were in public, I tried to be gay, and overacted my part. I knew I overacted; and I would be miserable for days afterwards. At last I became so unhappy that I could see no point in prolonging my existence. I began to think of suicide."

What happened to change this unhappy woman's life? Just a chance remark!

"A chance remark," Mrs. Allred continued, "transformed my whole life. My mother-in-law was talking one day of how she brought her children up, and she said, 'No matter what happened, I always insisted on their being themselves.' . . . 'On being themselves.' . . . That remark is what did it! In a flash, I realized I had brought all this misery on myself by trying to fit myself into a pattern to which I did not conform.

"I changed overnight! I started being myself. I tried to make a study of my own personality. Tried to find out *what I was*. I studied my strong points. I learned all I could about colors and styles, and dressed in a way that I felt was becoming to me. I reached out to make friends. I joined an organization—a small one at first—and was petrified with fright when they put me on a program. But each time I spoke, I gained a little courage. It took a long while—but today I have more happiness than I ever dreamed possible. In rearing my own children, I have always taught them the lesson I had to learn from such bitter experience: *No matter what happens, always be yourself!*"

This problem of being willing to be yourself is "as old as history," says Dr. James Gordon Gilkey, "and as universal as human life." This problem of being unwilling to be yourself is the hidden spring behind many neuroses and psychoses and complexes. Angelo Patri has written thirteen books and thousands of syndicated newspaper articles on the subject of child training, and he says: "Nobody is so miserable as he who longs to be somebody and something other than the person he is in body and mind."

This craving to be something you are not is especially rampant in Hollywood. The late Sam Wood, formerly one of Hollywood's best-known directors, said the greatest headache he had with aspiring young actors was exactly this problem: to make them be themselves. They all wanted to be second-rate Lana Turners or third-rate Clark Gables. "The public has already had that flavor," Sam Wood kept telling them; "now it wants something else."

Before he started directing such pictures as *Goodbye,*

Mr. Chips and *For Whom the Bell Tolls,* Sam Wood spent years in the real-estate business, developing sales personalities. He declared that the same principles apply in the business world as in the world of moving pictures. You won't get anywhere playing the ape. You can't be a parrot. "Experience has taught me," said Sam Wood, "that it is safest to drop, as quickly as possible, people who pretend to be what they aren't."

I recently asked Paul Boynton, employment director for the Socony-Vacuum Oil Company, what is the biggest mistake people make in applying for jobs. He ought to know: he has interviewed more than sixty thousand job seekers; and he has written a book entitled *6 Ways to Get a Job*. He replied: "The biggest mistake people make in applying for jobs is in not being themselves. Instead of taking their hair down and being completely frank, they often try to give you the answers they think you want." But it doesn't work, because nobody wants a phony. Nobody ever wants a counterfeit coin.

A certain daughter of a streetcar conductor had to learn that lesson the hard way. She longed to be a singer. But her face was her misfortune. She had a large mouth and protruding buck teeth. When she first sang in public—in a New Jersey night club—she tried to pull down her upper lip to cover her teeth. She tried to act "glamorous." The results? She made herself ridiculous. She was headed for failure.

However, there was a man in this night club who heard the girl sing and thought she had talent. "See here," he said bluntly, "I've been watching your performance and I know what it is you're trying to hide. You're ashamed of your teeth!" The girl was embarrassed, but the man continued, "What of it? Is there any particular crime in having buck teeth? Don't try to hide them! Open your mouth, and the audience will love you when they see you're not ashamed. Besides," he said shrewdly, "those teeth you're trying to hide may make your fortune!"

Cass Daley took his advice and forgot about her teeth. *From that time on*, she thought only about her audience. She opened her mouth wide and sang with such gusto and enjoyment that she became a top star in movies and radio. Other comedians are now trying to copy *her!*

The renowned William James was speaking of men who had never found themselves when he declared that the average man develops only ten per cent of his latent mental abilities. "Compared to what we ought to be," he wrote, "we are only half awake. We are making use of only a small part of our physical and mental resources. Stating the thing broadly, the human individual thus lives far within his limits. He possesses powers of various sorts which he habitually fails to use."

You and I have such abilities, so let's not waste a second worrying because we are not like other people. You are something new in this world. Never before, since the beginning of time, has there ever been anybody exactly like you; and never again throughout all the ages to come will there ever be anybody exactly like you again. The new science of genetics informs us that you are what you are largely as a result of twenty-four chromosomes contributed by your father and twenty-four chromosomes contributed by your mother. These forty-eight chromosomes comprise everything that determines what you inherit. In each chromosome there may be, says Amram Scheinfeld, "anywhere from scores to hundreds of genes —with a single gene, in some cases, able to change the whole life of an individual." Truly, we are "fearfully and wonderfully" made.

Even after your mother and father met and mated, there was only one chance in 300,000 billion that the person who is specifically you would be born! In other words, if you had 300,000 billion brothers and sisters, they might have all been different from you. Is all this guesswork? No. It it a scientific fact. If you would like to read more about it, go to your public library and borrow a book entitled *You and Heredity,* by Amram Scheinfeld.

I can talk with conviction about this subject of being yourself because I feel deeply about it. I know what I am talking about. I know from bitter and costly experience. To illustrate: when I first came to New York from the cornfields of Missouri, I enrolled in the American Academy of Dramatic Arts. I aspired to be an actor. I had what I thought was a brilliant idea, a short cut to success, an idea so simple, so foolproof, that I couldn't understand why thousands of ambitious people hadn't already discovered it. It was this: I would study how the famous actors of that day—John Drew, Walter Hampden, and Otis Skinner—got their effects. Then I would imitate the best points of each one of them and make myself into a shining, triumphant combination of all of them. How silly! How absurd! I had to waste years of my life imitating other people before it penetrated through my thick Missouri skull that I had to be myself, and that I couldn't possibly be anyone else.

That distressing experience ought to have taught me a lasting lesson. But it didn't. Not me. I was too dumb. I had to learn it all over again. Several years later, I set out to write what I hoped would be the best book on public speaking for businessmen that had ever been written. I had the same foolish idea about writing this book that I had formerly had about acting: I was going to *borrow* the ideas of a lot of other writers and put them all in one book—a book that would have everything. So I got scores of books on public speaking and spent a year incorporating their ideas into my manuscript. But it finally dawned on me once again that I was playing the fool. This hodgepodge of other men's ideas that I had written was so synthetic, so dull, that no businessman would ever plod through it. So I tossed a year's work into the wastebasket, and started all over again. This time I said to myself: "You've got to be Dale Carnegie, with all his faults and limitations. You can't possibly be anybody else." So I quit trying to be a combination of other men, and rolled up my sleeves and did what I should have done in the first place: I wrote a textbook on public speaking out of my own experiences, observations, and convictions as a speaker and a teacher of speaking. I learned—for all time, I hope—the lesson that Sir Walter Raleigh learned. (I am *not* talking about the Sir Walter who threw his coat in the mud for the Queen to step on. I am talking about the Sir Walter Raleigh who was professor of English literature at Oxford back in 1904.) "I can't write a book commensurate with Shakespeare," he said, "but I can write a book by me."

Be yourself. Act on the sage advice that Irving Berlin gave the late George Gershwin. When Berlin and Gershwin first met, Berlin was famous but Gershwin was a struggling young composer working for thirty-five dollars a week in Tin Pan Alley. Berlin, impressed by Gershwin's ability, offered Gershwin a job as his musical secretary at almost three times the salary he was then getting. "But don't take the job," Berlin advised. "If you do, you may develop into a second-rate Berlin. But if you insist on being yourself, someday you'll become a first-rate Gershwin."

Gershwin heeded that warning and slowly transformed himself into one of the significant American composers of his generation.

Charlie Chaplin, Will Rogers, Mary Margaret McBride, Gene Autry, and millions of others had to learn the lesson I am trying to hammer home in this chapter. They had to learn the hard way—just as I did.

When Charlie Chaplin first started making films, the director of the pictures insisted on Chaplin's imitating a popular German comedian of that day. Charlie Chaplin got nowhere until he acted himself. Bob Hope had a similar experience: spent years in a singing-and-dancing act—and got nowhere until he began to wisecrack and be himself. Will Rogers twirled a rope in vaudeville for years without saying a word. He got nowhere until he discovered his unique gift for humor and began to talk as he twirled his rope.

When Mary Margaret McBride first went on the air, she tried to be an Irish comedian and failed. When she tried to be just what she was—a plain country girl from Missouri—she became one of the most popular radio stars in New York.

When Gene Autry tried to get rid of his Texas accent and dressed like city boys and claimed he was from New York, people merely laughed behind his back. But when he started twanging his banjo and singing cowboy ballads, Gene Autry started out on a career that made him the world's most popular cowboy both in pictures and on the radio.

You are something new in this world. Be glad of it. Make the most of what nature gave you. In the last analysis, all art is autobiographical. You can sing only what you are. You can paint only what you are. You must be what your experiences, your environment, and your heredity have made you. For better or for worse, you must cultivate your own little garden. For better or for worse, you must play your own little instrument in the orchestra of life.

As Emerson said in his essay on "Self-Reliance": "There is a time in every man's education when he arrives at the conviction that envy is ignorance; that imitation is suicide; that he must take himself for better, for worse, as his portion; that though the wide universe is full of good, no kernel of nourishing corn can come to him but through his toil bestowed on that plot of ground which is given him to till. The power which resides in him is new in nature, and none but he knows what that is which he can do, nor does he know until he has tried."

That is the way Emerson said it. But here is the way a poet—the late Douglas Malloch—said it:

> If you can't be a pine on the top of the hill,
>   Be a scrub in the valley—but be
> The best little scrub by the side of the rill;
>   Be a bush, if you can't be a tree.
>
> If you can't be a bush, be a bit of the grass,
>   And some highway happier make;
> If you can't be a muskie, then just be a bass-
>   But the liveliest bass in the lake!
>
> We can't all be captains, we've got to be crew,
>   There's something for all of us here.
> There's big work to do and there's lesser to do
>   And the task we must do is the near.
>
> If you can't be a highway, then just be a trail,
>   If you can't be the sun, be a star;

It isn't by size that you win or you fail—
Be the best of whatever you are!

To cultivate a mental attitude that will bring us peace and freedom from worry, here is the rule:

Let's not imitate others. Let's find ourselves and be ourselves.

Chapter 2

FOUR GOOD WORKING HABITS THAT WILL
HELP PREVENT FATIGUE AND WORRY

Good Working Habit No. 1: *Clear Your Desk of All Papers Except Those Relating to the Immediate Problem at Hand.*

Roland L. Williams, President of Chicago and Northwestern Railway, says, "A person with his desk piled high with papers on various matters will find his work much easier and more accurate if he clears that desk of all but the immediate problem on hand. I call this good housekeeping, and it is the number-one step toward efficiency."

If you visit the Library of Congress in Washington, D. C., you will find five words painted on the ceiling—five words written by the poet Pope:

"Order is Heaven's first law."

Order ought to be the first law of business, too. But is it? No, the average businessman's desk is cluttered up with papers that he hasn't looked at for weeks. In fact, the publisher of a New Orleans newspaper once told me that his secretary cleared up one of his desks and found a typewriter that had been missing for two years!

The mere sight of a desk littered with unanswered mail and reports and memos is enough to breed confusion, tension, and worries. It is much worse than that. The constant reminder of "a million things to do and no time to do them" can worry you not only into tension and fatigue, but it can also worry you into high blood pressure, heart trouble, and stomach ulcers.

Dr. John H. Stokes, professor, Graduate School of Medicine, University of Pennsylvania, read a paper before the National Convention of the American Medical Association—a paper entitled "Functional Neuroses as

Complications of Organic Disease." In that paper, Dr. Stokes listed eleven conditions under the title: "What to Look for in the Patient's State of Mind." Here is the first item on that list:

"The sense of must or obligation; the unending stretch of things ahead that simply have to be done."

But how can such an elementary procedure as clearing your desk and making decisions help you avoid this high pressure, this sense of *must,* this sense of an "unending stretch of things ahead that simply have to be done"? Dr. William L. Sadler, the famous psychiatrist, tells of a patient who, by using this simple device, avoided a nervous breakdown. The man was an executive in a big Chicago firm. When he came to Dr. Sadler's office, he was tense, nervous, worried. He knew he was heading for a tailspin, but he couldn't quit work. He had to have help.

"While this man was telling me his story," Dr. Sadler says, "my telephone rang. It was the hospital calling; and, instead of deferring the matter, I took time right then to come to a decision. I always settle questions, if possible, right on the spot. I had no sooner hung up than the phone rang again. Again an urgent matter, which I took time to discuss. The third interruption came when a colleague of mine came to my office for advice on a patient who was critically ill. When I had finished with him, I turned to my caller and began to apologize for keeping him waiting. But he had brightened up. He had a completely different look on his face."

"Don't apologize, doctor!" this man said to Sadler. "In the last ten minutes, I think I've got a hunch as to what is wrong with me. I'm going back to my office and revise my working habits. . . . But before I go, do you mind if I take a look in your desk?"

Dr. Sadler opened up the drawers of his desk. All empty—except for supplies. "Tell me," said the patient, "where do you keep your unfinished business?"

"Finished!" said Sadler.

"And where do you keep your unanswered mail?"

"Answered!" Sadler told him. "My rule is never to lay down a letter until I have answered it. I dictate the reply to my secretary at once."

Six weeks later, this same executive invited Dr. Sadler to come to his office. He was changed—and so was his desk. He opened the desk drawers to show there was no unfinished business inside of the desk. "Six weeks ago," this executive said, "I had three different desks in two different offices—and was snowed under by my work. I was never finished. After talking to you, I came back here and cleared out a wagonload of reports and old papers. Now I work at one desk, settle things as they come up, and don't have a mountain of unfinished business nagging at me and making me tense and worried. But the most astonishing thing is I've recovered completely. There is nothing wrong any more with my health!"

Charles Evans Hughes, former Chief Justice of the United States Supreme Court, said: "Men do not die from overwork. They die from dissipation and worry." Yes, from dissipation of their energies—and worry because they never seem to get their work done.

Good Working Habit No. 2: *Do Things in the Order of Their Importance.*

Henry L. Doherty, founder of the nation-wide Cities Service Company, said that regardless of how much salary he paid, there were two abilities he found it almost impossible to find.

Those two priceless abilities: First, the ability to think. Second, the ability to do things in the order of their importance.

Charles Luckman, the lad who started from scratch and climbed in twelve years to president of the Pepsodent Company, got a salary of a hundred thousand dollars a year, and made a million dollars besides—that lad declares that he owes much of his success to developing the two abilities that Henry L. Doherty said he found almost impossible to find. Charles Luckman said: "As far back as I can remember, I have gotten up at five o'clock in the morning because I can think better then than any other time—I can think better then and plan my day, plan to do things in the order of their importance."

Frank Bettger, one of America's most successful insurance salesmen, doesn't wait until five o'clock in the morning to plan his day. He plans it the night before— sets a goal for himself—a goal to sell a certain amount of insurance that day. If he fails, that amount is added to the next day—and so on.

I know from long experience that one is not always able to do things in the order of their importance, but I also know that some kind of plan to do first things first is infinitely better than extemporizing as you go along.

If George Bernard Shaw had not made it a rigid rule to do first things first, he would probably have failed as a writer and might have remained a bank cashier all his life. His plan called for writing five pages each day. That plan inspired him to go right on writing five pages a day for nine heartbreaking years, even though he made a total of only thirty dollars in those nine years—about a penny a day. Even Robinson Crusoe wrote out a schedule of what he would do each hour of the day.

Good Working Habit No. 3: *When You Face a Problem, Solve It Then and There if You Have the Facts Necessary to Make a Decision. Don't Keep Putting Off Decisions.*

One of my former students, the late H. P. Howell, told me that when he was a member of the board of directors of U. S. Steel, the meetings of the board were often long-drawn-out affairs—many problems were discussed, few decisions were made. The result: each member of the board had to carry home bundles of reports to study.

Finally, Mr. Howell persuaded the board of directors to take up one problem at a time and come to a decision. No procrastination—no putting off. The decision might be to ask for additional facts; it might be to do something or do nothing. But a decision was reached on each problem before passing on to the next. Mr. Howell told me that the results were striking and salutary: the docket was cleared. The calendar was clean. No longer was it necessary for each member to carry home a bundle of reports. No longer was there a worried sense of unresolved problems.

A good rule, not only for the board of directors of U. S. Steel, but for you and me.

Good Working Habit No. 4: *Learn to Organize, Deputize, and Supervise.*

Many a businessman is driving himself to a premature grave because he has never learned to delegate responsibility to others, insists on doing everything himself. Result: details and confusion overwhelm him. He is driven by a sense of hurry, worry, anxiety, and tension. It is hard to learn to delegate responsibilities. I know. It was hard for me, awfully hard. I also know from experience the disasters that can be caused by delegating authority to the wrong people. But difficult as it is to delegate authority, the executive must do it if he is to avoid worry, tension, and fatigue.

The man who builds up a big business, and doesn't learn to organize, deputize, and supervise, usually pops off with heart trouble in his fifties or early sixties—heart trouble caused by tension and worries. Want a specific instance? Look at the death notices in your local paper.

Chapter 3

WHAT MAKES YOU TIRED—AND WHAT
YOU CAN DO ABOUT IT

Here is an outstanding and significant fact: Mental work alone can't make you tired. Sounds absurd. But a few years ago, scientists tried to find out how long the human brain could labor without reaching "a diminished capacity for work," the scientific definition of fatigue. To the amazement of these scientists, they discovered that blood passing through the brain, when it is active, shows no fatigue at all! If you took blood from the veins of a day laborer while he was working, you would find it full of "fatigue toxins" and fatigue products. But if you took a drop of blood from the brain of an Albert Einstein, it would show no fatigue toxins whatever at the end of the day.

So far as the brain is concerned, it can work "as well and as swiftly at the end of eight or even twelve hours of effort as at the beginning." The brain is utterly tireless. . . . So what makes you tired?

Psychiatrists declare that most of our fatigue derives from our mental and emotional attitudes. One of England's most distinguished psychiatrists, J. A. Hadfield, says in his book *The Psychology of Power,* "the greater part of the fatigue from which we suffer is of mental origin; in fact exhaustion of purely physical origin is rare."

One of America's most distinguished psychiatrists, Dr. A. A. Brill, goes even further. He declares, "One hundred per cent of the fatigue of the sedentary worker in good health is due to psychological factors, by which we mean emotional factors."

What kinds of emotional factors tire the sedentary (or

27

sitting) worker? Joy? Contentment? No! Never! Boredom, resentment, a feeling of not being appreciated, a feeling of futility, hurry, anxiety, worry—those are the emotional factors that exhaust the sitting worker, make him susceptible to colds, reduce his output, and send him home with a nervous headache. Yes, we get tired because our emotions produce nervous tensions in the body.

The Metropolitan Life Insurance Company pointed that out in a leaflet on fatigue: "Hard work by itself," says this great life insurance company, "seldom causes fatigue which cannot be cured by a good sleep or rest. . . . Worry, tenseness, and emotional upsets are three of the biggest causes of fatigue. Often they are to blame when physical or mental work seems to be the cause. . . . Remember that a tense muscle is a working muscle. Ease up! Save energy for important duties."

Stop now, right where you are, and give yourself a checkup. As you read these lines, are you scowling at the book? Do you feel a strain between the eyes? Are you sitting relaxed in your chair? Or are you hunching up your shoulders? Are the muscles of your face tense? Unless your entire body is as limp and relaxed as an old rag doll, you are at this very moment producing nervous tensions and muscular tensions. *You are producing nervous tensions and nervous fatigue!*

Why do we produce these unnecessary tensions in doing mental work? Josselyn says: "I find that the chief obstacle . . . is the almost universal belief that hard work requires a feeling of effort, else it is not well done." So we scowl when we concentrate. We hunch up our shoulders. We call on our muscles to make the motion of *effort*, which in no way assists our brain in its work.

Here is an astonishing and tragic truth: millions of people who wouldn't dream of wasting dollars go right on wasting and squandering their energy with the recklessness of seven drunken sailors in Singapore.

What is the answer to this nervous fatigue? Relax! Relax! Relax! *Learn to relax while you are doing your work!*

Easy? No. You will probably have to reverse the habits of a lifetime. But it is worth the effort, for it may revolutionize your life! William James said, in his essay "The Gospel of Relaxation": "The American overtension and jerkiness and breathlessness and intensity and agony of expression . . . are *bad habits,* nothing more or less." *Tension is a habit. Relaxing is a habit. And bad habits can be broken, good habits formed.*

How do you relax? Do you start with your mind, or do you start with your nerves? You don't start with either. You always begin to *relax with your muscles!*

Let's give it a try. To show how it is done, suppose we start with your eyes. Read this paragraph through, and when you've reached the end, lean back, close your eyes, *and say to your eyes* silently, "Let go. Let go. Stop straining, stop frowning. Let go. Let go." Repeat that over and over very slowly for a minute. . . .

Didn't you notice that after a few seconds the muscles of the eyes *began to obey?* Didn't you feel as though some hand had wiped away the tension? Well, incredible as it seems, you have sampled in that one minute the whole key and secret to the art of relaxing. You can do the same thing with the jaw, with the muscles of the face, with the neck, with the shoulders, the whole of the body. But the most important organ of all is the eye. Dr. Edmund Jacobson of the University of Chicago has gone so far as to say that if you can completely relax the muscles of the eyes, you can forget all your troubles! The reason the eyes are so important in relieving nervous tension is that they burn up one fourth of all the nervous energies consumed by the body. That is also why so many people with perfectly sound vision suffer from "eyestrain." They are tensing the eyes.

Vicki Baum, the famous novelist, says that when she was a child, she met an old man who taught her one of the most important lessons she ever learned. She had fallen down and cut her knees and hurt her wrist. The old man picked her up; he had once been a circus clown; and, as he brushed her off, he said: "The reason you injured yourself was because you don't know how to relax. You have to pretend you are as limp as a sock, as an old crumpled sock. Come, I'll show you how to do it."

That old man taught Vicki Baum and the other children how to fall, how to do flip-flops, and how to turn somersaults. And always he insisted, "Think of yourself as an old crumpled sock. Then you've *got* to relax!"

You can relax in odd moments, almost anywhere you are. Only don't make an effort to relax. *Relaxation is the absence of all tension and effort.* Think ease and relaxation. Begin by thinking relaxation of the muscles of your eyes and your face, saying over and over, "Let go . . . let go . . . let go and relax." Feel the energy flowing out of your facial muscles to the center of your body. Think of yourself as free from tension as a baby.

That is what Galli-Curci, the great soprano, used to do. Helen Jepson told me that she used to see Galli-Curci before a performance, sitting in a chair with all her muscles relaxed and her lower jaw so limp it actually sagged. An excellent practice—it kept her from becoming too nervous before her stage entrance; it prevented fatigue.

Here are five suggestions that will help you learn to relax:

1. Read one of the best books ever written on this subject: *Release from Nervous Tension,* by Dr. David Harold Fink. Most public libraries have it. If you wish to own a copy, order one from your local bookstore or send an order and $4.50 to the publishers: Simon and Schuster, 630 Fifth Avenue, New York, New York 10020. I also urge you to read *Why Be Tired,* by Daniel W. Josselyn. (If you can't find it in your public library, you may order a copy from Doubleday Bookstore, 673 Fifth Ave., New York, New York 10022.

2. Relax in odd moments. Let your body go limp like an old sock. I keep an old, maroon-colored sock on my desk as I work—keep it there as a reminder of how limp I ought to be. If you haven't got

a sock, a cat will do. Did you ever pick up a kitten sleeping in the sunshine? If so, both ends sagged like a wet newspaper. Even the yogis in India say that if you want to master the art of relaxation, study the cat. I never saw a tired cat, a cat with a nervous breakdown, or a cat suffering from insomnia, worry, or stomach ulcers. You will probably avoid these disasters if you learn to relax as the cat does.

3. Work, as much as possible, in a comfortable position. Remember that tensions on the body produce aching shoulders and nervous fatigue.

4. Check yourself four or five times a day, and say to yourself, "Am I making my work harder than it actually is? Am I using muscles that have nothing to do with the work I am doing?" This will help you form the *habit* of relaxing, and as Dr. David Harold Fink says, "Among those who know psychology best, it is habits two to one."

5. Test yourself again at the end of the day, by asking yourself, "Just how tired am I? If I am tired, it is not because of the mental work I have done but because of the way I have done it." "I measure my accomplishments," says Daniel W. Josselyn, "not by how tired I am at the end of the day, but how tired I am not." He says, "When I feel particularly tired at the end of the day, or when irritability proves that my nerves are tired, I know beyond question that it has been an inefficient day both as to quantity and quality." If every businessman in America would learn that same lesson, our death rate from "hypertension" diseases would drop overnight. And we would stop filling up our sanitariums and asylums with men who have been broken by fatigue and worry.

Chapter 4

HOW TO BANISH THE BOREDOM THAT
PRODUCES FATIGUE, WORRY,
AND RESENTMENT

One of the chief causes of fatigue is boredom. To illustrate, let's take the case of Alice, a stenographer who lives on your street. Alice came home one night utterly exhausted. She *acted* fatigued. She *was* fatigued. She had a headache. She had a backache. She was so exhausted she wanted to go to bed without waiting for dinner. Her mother pleaded. . . . She sat down at the table. The telephone rang. The boy friend! An invitation to a dance! Her eyes sparkled. Her spirits soared. She rushed upstairs, put on her Alice-blue gown, and danced until three o'clock in the morning; and when she finally did get home, she was not the slightest bit exhausted. She was, in fact, so exhilarated she couldn't fall asleep.

Was Alice really and honestly tired eight hours earlier, when she looked and acted exhausted? Sure she was. She was exhausted because she was bored with her work, perhaps bored with life. There are millions of Alices. You may be one of them.

It is a well-known fact that your emotional attitude usually has far more to do with producing fatigue than has physical exertion. A few years ago, Joseph E. Barmack, Ph.D., published in the *Archives of Psychology* a report of some of his experiments showing how boredom produces fatigue. Dr. Barmack put a group of students through a series of tests in which, he knew, they could have little interest. The result? The students felt tired and sleepy, complained of headaches and eyestrain, felt irritable. In some cases, even their stomachs were upset. Was it all "imagination"? No. Metabolism tests were taken of these students. These tests showed that the blood pressure of the body and the consumption of oxygen actually decrease when a person is bored, and that the whole metabolism picks up immediately as soon as he begins to feel interest and pleasure in his work!

We rarely get tired when we are doing something interesting and exciting. For example, I recently took a vacation in the Canadian Rockies up around Lake Louise. I spent several days trout fishing along Corral Creek, fighting my way through brush higher than my head, stumbling over logs, struggling through fallen timber— yet after eight hours of this, I was not exhausted. Why? Because I was excited, exhilarated. I had a sense of high achievement: six cut-throat trout. But suppose I had been bored by fishing, then how do you think I would have felt? I would have been worn out by such strenuous work at an altitude of seven thousand feet.

Even in such exhausting activities as mountain climbing, boredom may tire you far more than the strenuous work involved. For example, Mr. S. H. Kingman, president of the Farmers and Mechanics Savings Bank of Minneapolis, told me of an incident that is a perfect illustration of that statement. In July, 1943, the Canadian government asked the Canadian Alpine Club to furnish guides to train the members of the Prince of Wales Rangers in mountain climbing. Mr. Kingman was one of the guides chosen to train these soldiers. He told me how he and the other guides—men ranging from forty-two to fifty-nine years of age—took these young army men on long hikes across glaciers and snow fields and up a sheer cliff of forty feet, where they had to climb with ropes and tiny footholds and precarious handholds. They climbed Michael's Peak, the Vice-President Peak, and other unnamed peaks in the Little Yoho Valley in the Canadian Rockies. After fifteen hours of mountain climbing, these young men, who were in the pink of condition (they had just finished a six-week course in tough Commando training), were utterly exhausted.

Was their fatigue caused by using muscles that had not been hardened by Commando training? Any man who had ever been through Commando training would hoot at such a ridiculous question! No, they were utterly exhausted because they were bored by mountain climbing. They were so tired that many of them fell asleep without waiting to eat. But the guides—men who were two and three times as old as the soldiers—were they tired? Yes, but not exhausted. The guides ate dinner and stayed up for hours, talking about the day's experiences. They were not exhausted because they were interested.

When Dr. Edward Thorndike of Columbia was conducting experiments in fatigue, he kept young men awake for almost a week by keeping them constantly interested. After much investigation, Dr. Thorndike is reported to have said: "Boredom is the only real cause of diminution of work."

If you are a mental worker, it is seldom the amount of work you do that makes you tired. You may be tired by the amount of work you do *not* do. For example, remember the day last week when you were constantly interrupted. No letters answered. Appointments broken. Trouble here and there. Everything went wrong that day. You accomplished nothing whatever, yet you went home exhausted—and with a splitting head.

The next day everything clicked at the office. You accomplished forty times more than you did the previous day. Yet you went home fresh as a snowy-white gardenia. You have had that experience. So have I.

The lesson to be learned? Just this: our fatigue is often caused not by work, but by worry, frustration, and resentment.

While writing this chapter, I went to see a revival of Jerome Kern's delightful musical comedy, *Show Boat.* Captain Andy, captain of the *Cotton Blossom,* says in one of his philosophical interludes: "The lucky folks are the ones that get to do things they enjoy doing." Such folk are lucky because they have more energy, more happiness, less worry, and less fatigue. Where your interests are, there is your energy also. Walking ten blocks with a nagging wife can be more fatiguing than walking ten miles with an adoring sweetheart.

And so what? What can you do about it? Well, here is what one stenographer did about it—a stenographer working for an oil company in Tulsa, Oklahoma. For several days each month, she had one of the dullest jobs imaginable: filling out printed forms for oil leases, inserting figures and statistics. This task was so boring that she resolved, in self-defense, to make it interesting. How? She had a daily contest with herself. She counted the number of forms she filled out each morning, and then tried to excel that record in the afternoon. She counted each day's total and tried to better it the next day. Result? She was soon able to fill out more of these dull printed forms than any other stenographer in her division. And what did all this get her? Praise? No. . . . Thanks? No. . . . Promotion? No. . . . Increased pay? No. . . . But it did help to prevent the fatigue that is spawned by boredom. It did give her a mental stimulant. Because she had done her best to make a dull job interesting, she had more energy, more zest, and got far more happiness out of her leisure hours.

I happen to know this story is true, because I married that girl.

Here is the story of another stenographer who found it paid to act *as if* her work were interesting. She used to fight her work. But no more. Her name is Miss Vallie G. Golden, and she lives at 473 South Kenilworth Avenue, Elmhurst, Illinois. Here is her story, as she wrote it to me:

"There are four stenographers in my office and each of us is assigned to take letters from several men. Once in a while we get jammed up in these assignments; and one day, when an assistant department head insisted that I do a long letter over, I started to rebel. I tried to point out to him that the letter could be corrected without being retyped—and he retorted that if I didn't do it over, he would find someone else who would! I was absolutely fuming! But as I started to retype this letter, it suddenly occurred to me that there were a lot of other people who would jump at the chance to do the work I was doing. Also, that I was being paid a salary to do just that work.

I began to feel better. I suddenly made up my mind to do my work as if I actually enjoyed it—even though I despised it. Then I made this important discovery: if I do my work *as if* I really enjoy it, then I do enjoy it to some extent. I also found I can work faster when I enjoy my work. So there is seldom any need now for me to work overtime. This new attitude of mine gained me the reputation of being a good worker. And when one of the department superintendents needed a private secretary, he asked for me for the job—because, he said, I was willing to do extra work without being sulky! This matter of the power of a changed mental attitude," wrote Miss Golden, "has been a tremendously important discovery to me. It has worked wonders!"

Miss Golden used the wonder-working *"as if"* philosophy of Professor Hans Vaihinger. He taught us to act *"as if"* we were happy—and so on.

If you act *"as if"* you are interested in your job, that bit of acting will tend to make your interest real. It will also tend to decrease your fatigue, your tensions, and your worries.

A few years ago, Harlan A. Howard made a decision that completely altered his life. He resolved to make a dull job interesting—and he certainly had a dull one: washing plates, scrubbing counters, and dishing out ice cream in the high-school lunchroom while the other boys were playing ball or kidding the girls. Harlan Howard despised his job—but since he had to stick to it, he resolved to study ice cream—how it was made, what ingredients were used, why some ice creams were better than others. He studied the chemistry of ice cream, and became a whiz in the high-school chemistry course. He was so interested now in food chemistry that he entered the Massachusetts State College and majored in the field of "food technology." When the New York Cocoa Exchange offered a hundred-dollar prize for the best paper on uses of cocoa and chocolate—a prize open to all college students—who do you suppose won it? . . . That's right. Harlan Howard.

When he found it difficult to get a job, he opened a

private laboratory in the basement of his home at 750 North Pleasant Street, Amherst, Massachusetts. Shortly after that, a new law was passed. The bacteria in milk had to be counted. Harlan A. Howard was soon counting bacteria for the fourteen milk companies in Amherst—and he had to hire two assistants.

Where will he be twenty-five years from now? Well, the men who are now running the business of food chemistry will be retired then, or dead; and their places will be taken by young lads who are now radiating initiative and enthusiasm. Twenty-five years from now, Harlan A. Howard will probably be one of the leaders in his profession, while some of his classmates to whom he used to sell ice cream over the counter will be sour, unemployed, cussing the government, and complaining that they never had a chance. Harlan A. Howard might never have had a chance, either, if he hadn't resolved to make a dull job interesting.

Years ago, there was another young man who was bored with his dull job of standing at a lathe, turning out bolts in a factory. His first name was Sam. Sam wanted to quit, but he was afraid he couldn't find another job. Since he had to do this dull work, Sam decided he would make it interesting. So he ran a race with the mechanic operating a machine beside him. One of them was to trim off the rough surfaces on his machine, and the other was to trim the bolts down to the proper diameter. They would switch machines occasionally and see who could turn out the most bolts. The foreman, impressed with Sam's speed and accuracy, soon gave him a better job. That was the start of a whole series of promotions. Thirty years later, Sam—Samuel Vauclain—was president of the Baldwin Locomotive Works. But he might have remained a mechanic all his life if he had not resolved to make a dull job interesting.

H. V. Kaltenborn—the famous radio news analyst—once told me how he made a dull job interesting. When he was twenty-two years old, he worked his way across the Atlantic on a cattle boat, feeding and watering the steers. After making a bicycle tour of England, he arrived in Paris, hungry and broke. Pawning his camera for five dollars, he put an ad in the Paris edition of *The New York Herald* and got a job selling stereopticon machines. If you are old enough, you may remember those old-fashioned stereoscopes that we used to hold up before our eyes to look at two pictures exactly alike. As we looked, a miracle happened. The two lenses in the stereoscope transformed the two pictures into a single scene with the effect of a third dimension. We saw distance. We got an astounding sense of perspective.

Well, as I was saying, Kaltenborn started out selling these machines from door to door in Paris—and he couldn't speak French. But he earned five thousand dollars in commissions the first year, and made himself one of the highest-paid salesmen in France that year. H. V. Kaltenborn told me that this experience did as much to develop within him the qualities that make for success as did any single year of study at Harvard. Confidence? He told me himself that after that experience, he felt he could have sold *The Congressional Record* to French housewives.

That experience gave him an intimate understanding of French life that later proved invaluable in interpreting, on the radio, European events.

How did he manage to become an expert salesman when he couldn't speak French? Well, he had his employer write out his sales talk in perfect French, and he memorized it. He would ring a doorbell, a housewife would answer, and Kaltenborn would begin repeating his memorized sales talk with an accent so terrible it was funny. He would show the housewife his pictures, and when she asked a question, he would shrug his shoulders and say, "An American . . . an American." He would then take off his hat and point to a copy of the sales talk in perfect French that he had pasted in the top of his hat. The housewife would laugh, he would laugh —and show her more pictures. When H. V. Kaltenborn told me about this, he confessed that the job had been far from easy. He told me that there was only one quality that pulled him through: his determination to make the job interesting. Every morning before he started out, he looked into the mirror and gave himself a pep talk: "Kaltenborn, *you have to do this if you want to eat. Since you have to do it—why not have a good time doing it? Why not imagine every time you ring a doorbell that you are an actor before the footlights and that there's an audience out there looking at you? After all, what you are doing is just as funny as something on the stage. So why not put a lot of zest and enthusiasm into it?"*

Mr. Kaltenborn told me that these daily pep talks helped him transform a task that he had once hated and dreaded into an adventure that he liked and made highly profitable.

When I asked Mr. Kaltenborn if he had any advice to give to the young men of America who are eager to succeed, he said: "Yes, go to bat with yourself every morning. We talk a lot about the importance of physical exercise to wake us up out of the half-sleep in which so many of us walk around. But we need, even more, some spiritual and mental exercises every morning to stir us into action. Give yourself a pep talk every day."

Is giving yourself a pep talk every day silly, superficial, childish? No, on the contrary, it is the very essence of sound psychology. "Our life is what our thoughts make it." These words are just as true today as they were eighteen centuries ago when Marcus Aurelius first wrote them in his book of *Meditations:* "Our life is what our thoughts make it."

By talking to yourself every hour of the day, you can direct yourself to think thoughts of courage and happiness, thoughts of power and peace. By talking to yourself about the things you have to be grateful for, you can fill your mind with thoughts that soar and sing.

By thinking the right thoughts, you can make any job less distasteful. Your boss wants you to be interested in your job so that he will make more money. But let's forget about what the boss wants. Think only of what getting interested in your job will do for you. Remind yourself that it may double the amount of happiness you get out of life, for you spend about one half of your waking hours at your work, and if you don't find happiness in your work, you may never find it anywhere. Keep reminding yourself that getting interested in your job will take your mind off your worries, and, in the long run, will probably bring promotion and increased pay. Even if it doesn't do that, it will reduce fatigue to a minimum and help you enjoy your hours of leisure.

Chapter 5

WOULD YOU TAKE A MILLION DOLLARS
FOR WHAT YOU HAVE?

I have known Harold Abbott for years. He lives at 820 South Madison Avenue, Webb City, Missouri. He used to be my lecture manager. One day he and I met in Kansas City and he drove me down to my farm at Belton, Missouri. During that drive, I asked him how he kept from worrying; and he told me an inspiring story that I shall never forget.

"I used to worry a lot," he said, "but one spring day in 1934, I was walking down West Dougherty Street in Webb City when I saw a sight that banished all my worries. It all happened in ten seconds, but during those ten seconds I learned more about how to live than I had learned in the previous ten years. For two years I had been running a grocery store in Webb City," Harold Abbott said, as he told me the story. "I had not only lost all my savings, but I had incurred debts that took me seven years to pay back. My grocery store had been closed the previous Saturday; and now I was going to the Merchants and Miners Bank to borrow money so I could go to Kansas City to look for a job. I walked like a beaten man. I had lost all my fight and faith. Then suddenly I saw coming down the street a man who had no legs. He was sitting on a little wooden platform equipped with wheels from roller skates. He propelled himself along the street with a block of wood in each hand. I met him just after he had crossed the street and was starting to lift himself up a few inches over the curb to the sidewalk. As he tilted his little wooden platform to an angle, his eyes met mine. He greeted me with a grand smile. 'Good morning, sir. It is a fine morning, isn't it?' he said with spirit.

41

As I stood looking at him, I realized how rich I was. I had two legs. I could walk. I felt ashamed of my self-pity. I said to myself if he can be happy, cheerful, and confident without legs, I certainly can with legs. I could already feel my chest lifting. I had intended to ask the Merchants and Miners Bank for only one hundred dollars. But now I had courage to ask for *two* hundred. I had intended to say that I wanted to go to Kansas City to *try* to get a job. But now I announced confidently that I wanted to go to Kansas City to *get* a job. I got the loan; and I got the job.

"I now have the following words pasted on my bathroom mirror, and I read them every morning as I shave:

> *I had the blues because I had no shoes,*
> *Until upon the street, I met a man who had no feet.*"

I once asked Eddie Rickenbacker what was the biggest lesson he had learned from drifting about with his companions in life rafts for twenty-one days, hopelessly lost in the Pacific. "The biggest lesson I learned from that experience," he said, "was that if you have all the fresh water you want to drink and all the food you want to eat, you ought never to complain about anything."

Time ran an article about a sergeant who had been wounded on Guadalcanal. Hit in the throat by a shell fragment, this sergeant had had seven blood transfusions. Writing a note to his doctor, he asked: "Will I live?" The doctor replied: "Yes." He wrote another note, asking: "Will I be able to talk?" Again the answer was yes. He then wrote another note, saying: *"Then what in the hell am I worrying about?"*

Why don't you stop right now and ask yourself: "What in the hell am I worrying about?" You will probably find that it is comparatively unimportant and insignificant.

About ninety per cent of the things in our lives are right and about ten per cent are wrong. If we want to be happy, all we have to do is to concentrate on the ninety per cent that are right and ignore the ten per cent that are wrong. If we want to be worried and bitter and have stomach ulcers, all we have to do is to concentrate on the ten per cent that are wrong and ignore the ninety per cent that are glorious.

The words "Think and Thank" are inscribed in many of the Cromwellian churches of England. These words ought to be inscribed on our hearts, too: "Think and Thank." Think of all we have to be grateful for, and thank God for all our boons and bounties.

Jonathan Swift, author of *Gulliver's Travels,* was the most devastating pessimist in English literature. He was so sorry that he had been born that he wore black and fasted on his birthdays; yet, in his despair, this supreme pessimist of English literature praised the great health-giving powers of cheerfulness and happiness. "The best doctors in the world," he declared, "are Doctor Diet, Doctor Quiet, and Doctor Merryman."

You and I may have the services of "Doctor Merryman" free every hour of the day by keeping our attention fixed on all the incredible riches we possess—riches exceeding by far the fabled treasures of Ali Baba. Would you sell both your eyes for a billion dollars? What would you take for your two legs? Your hands? Your hearing? Your children? Your family? Add up your assets, and you will find that you won't sell what you have for all the gold ever amassed by the Rockefellers, the Fords and the Morgans combined.

But do we appreciate all this? Ah, no. As Schopenhauer said: "We seldom think of what we have but always of what we lack." Yes, the tendency to "seldom think of what we have but always of what we lack" is the greatest tragedy on earth. It has probably caused more misery than all the wars and diseases in history.

It caused John Palmer to turn "from a regular guy into an old grouch," and almost wrecked his home. I know because he told me so.

Mr. Palmer lives at 30 19th Avenue, Paterson, New Jersey. "Shortly after I returned from the army," he said, "I started in business for myself. I worked hard day and night. Things were going nicely. Then trouble started. I couldn't get parts and materials. I was afraid

I would have to give up my business. I worried so much that I changed from a regular guy into an old grouch. I became so sour and cross that—well, I didn't know it then; but I now realize that I came very near to losing my happy home. Then one day a young, disabled veteran who works for me said, 'Johnny, you ought to be ashamed of yourself. You take on as if you were the only person in the world with troubles. Suppose you do have to shut up shop for a while—so what? You can start up again when things get normal. You've got a lot to be thankful for. Yet you are always growling. Boy, how I wish I were in your shoes! Look at me. I've got only one arm, and half of my face is shot away, and yet I am not complaining. If you don't stop your growling and grumbling, you will lose not only your business, but also your health, your home, and your friends!"

"Those remarks stopped me dead in my tracks. They made me realize how well off I was. I resolved then and there that I would change and be my old self again—and I did."

A friend of mine, Lucile Blake, had to tremble on the edge of tragedy before she learned to be happy about what she had instead of worrying over what she lacked.

I met Lucile years ago, when we were both studying short story writing in the Columbia University School of Journalism. Nine years ago, she got the shock of her life. She was living then in Tucson, Arizona. She had—well, here is the story as she told it to me:

"I had been living in a whirl: studying the organ at the University of Arizona, conducting a speech clinic in town, and teaching a class in musical appreciation at the Desert Willow Ranch, where I was staying. I was going in for parties, dances, horseback rides under the stars. One morning I collapsed. My heart! 'You will have to lie in bed for a year of complete rest,' the doctor said. He didn't encourage me to believe I would ever be strong again.

"In bed for a year! To be an invalid—perhaps to die! I was terror-stricken! Why did all this have to happen to me? What had I done to deserve it? I wept and wailed. I was bitter and rebellious. But I did go to bed as the doctor advised. A neighbor of mine, Mr. Rudolf, an artist, said to me, 'You think now that spending a year in bed will be a tragedy. But it won't be. You will have time to think and get acquainted with yourself. You will make more spiritual growth in these next few months than you have made during all your previous life.' I became calmer, and tried to develop a new sense of values. I read books of inspiration. One day I heard a radio commentator say: 'You can express only what is in your own consciousness.' I had heard words like these many times before, but now they reached down inside me and took root. I resolved to think only the thoughts I wanted to live by: thoughts of joy, happiness, health. I forced myself each morning, as soon as I awoke, to go over all the things I had to be grateful for. No pain. A lovely young daughter. My eyesight. My hearing. Lovely music on the radio. Time to read. Good food. Good friends. I was so cheerful and had so many visitors that the doctor put up a sign saying that only one visitor at a time would be allowed in my cabin—and only at certain hours.

"Nine years have passed since then, and I now lead a full, active life. I am deeply grateful now for that year I spent in bed. It was the most valuable and the happiest year I spent in Arizona. The habit I formed then of counting my blessings each morning still remains with me. It is one of my most precious possessions. I am ashamed to realize that I never really learned to live until I feared I was going to die."

My dear Lucile Blake, you may not realize it, but you learned the same lesson that Dr. Samuel Johnson learned two hundred years ago. "The habit of looking on the best side of every event," said Dr. Johnson, "is worth more than a thousand pounds a year."

Those words were uttered, mind you, not by a professional optimist, but by a man who had known anxiety, rags, and hunger for twenty years—and finally became one of the most eminent writers of his generation and the most celebrated conversationalist of all time.

Logan Pearsall Smith packed a lot of wisdom into a

few words when he said: "There are two things to aim
at in life: first, to get what you want; and, after that, to
enjoy it. Only the wisest of mankind achieve the second."

Would you like to know how to make even dishwashing
at the kitchen sink a thrilling experience? If so, read an
inspiring book of incredible courage by Borghild Dahl.
It is called *I Wanted to See*. You may borrow it from
your public library or purchase it from your local bookstore or from the publisher, The Macmillan Company,
60 Fifth Avenue, New York City. Price $4.95.

This book was written by a woman who was practically
blind for half a century. "I had only one eye," she writes,
"and it was so covered with dense scars that I had to do
all my seeing through one small opening in the left of
the eye. I could see a book only by holding it up close
to my face and by straining my one eye as hard as I
could to the left."

But she refused to be pitied, refused to be considered
"different." As a child, she wanted to play hopscotch
with other children, but she couldn't see the markings.
So after the other children had gone home, she got down
on the ground and crawled along with her eyes near to
the marks. She memorized every bit of the ground where
she and her friends played and soon became an expert
at running games. She did her reading at home, holding
a book of large print so close to her eyes that her eye-
lashes brushed the pages. She earned two college degrees:
an A.B. from the University of Minnesota and a Master
of Arts from Columbia University.

She started teaching in the tiny village of Twin Valley,
Minnesota, and rose until she became professor of journalism and literature at Augustana College in Sioux Falls,
South Dakota. She taught there for thirteen years, lectur-
ing before women's clubs and giving radio talks about
books and authors. "In the back of my mind," she writes,
"there had always lurked a fear of total blindness. In
order to overcome this, I had adopted a cheerful, almost
hilarious, attitude toward life."

Then in 1943, when she was fifty-two years old, a
miracle happened: an operation at the famous Mayo Clin-

ic. She could now see forty times as well as she had ever been able to see before.

A new and exciting world of loveliness opened before her. She now found it thrilling even to wash dishes in the kitchen sink. "I begin to play with the white fluffy suds in the dishpan," she writes. "I dip my hands into them and I pick up a ball of tiny soap bubbles. I hold them up against the light, and in each of them I can see the brilliant colors of a miniature rainbow."

As she looked through the window above the kitchen sink, she saw "the flapping gray-black wings of the sparrows flying through the thick, falling snow."

She found such ecstasy looking at the soap bubbles and sparrows that she closed her book with these words: " 'Dear Lord,' I whisper, 'Our Father in Heaven, I thank Thee. I thank Thee.' "

Imagine thanking God because you can wash dishes and see rainbows in bubbles and sparrows flying through the snow!

You ought and I ought to be ashamed of ourselves. All the days of our years we have been living in a fairyland of beauty, but we have been too blind to see, too satiated to enjoy.

If we want to stop worrying and start living, another rule is:

Count your blessings—not your troubles!

Chapter 6

REMEMBER THAT NO ONE EVER KICKS
A DEAD DOG

An event occurred in 1929 that created a national sensation in educational circles. Learned men from all over America rushed to Chicago to witness the affair. A few years earlier, a young man by the name of Robert Hutchins had worked his way through Yale, acting as a waiter, a lumberjack, a tutor, and a clothesline salesman. Now, only eight years later, he was being inaugurated as president of the fourth richest university in America, the University of Chicago. His age? Thirty. Incredible! The older educators shook their heads. Criticism came roaring down upon this "boy wonder" like a rockslide. He was this and he was that—too young, inexperienced—his educational ideas were cockeyed. Even the newspapers joined in the attack.

The day he was inaugurated, a friend said to the father of Robert Maynard Hutchins: "I was shocked this morning to read that newspaper editorial denouncing your son."

"Yes," the elder Hutchins replied, "it was severe, but remember that no one ever kicks a dead dog."

Yes, and the more important a dog is, the more satisfaction people get in kicking him. The Prince of Wales who later became Edward VIII (now Duke of Windsor) had that brought home to him in the seat of his pants. He was attending Dartmouth College in Devonshire at the time—a college that corresponds to our Naval Academy at Annapolis. The Prince was about fourteen. One day one of the naval officers found him crying, and asked him what was wrong. He refused to tell at first, but finally admitted the truth: he was being kicked by the naval cadets. The commodore of the college summoned the boys and

48

explained to them that the Prince had not complained, but he wanted to find out why the Prince had been singled out for this rough treatment.

After much hemming and hawing and toe scraping, the cadets finally confessed that when they themselves became commanders and captains in the King's Navy, they wanted to be able to say that they had kicked the King!

So when you are kicked and criticized, remember that it is often done because it gives the kicker a feeling of importance. It often means that you are accomplishing something and are worthy of attention. Many people get a sense of savage satisfaction out of denouncing those who are better educated than they are or more successful. For example, while I was writing this chapter, I received a letter from a woman denouncing General William Booth, founder of the Salvation Army. I had given a laudatory broadcast about General Booth; so this woman wrote me, saying that General Booth had stolen eight million dollars of the money he had collected to help poor people. The charge, of course, was absurd. But this woman wasn't looking for truth. She was seeking the mean-spirited gratification that she got from tearing down someone far above her. I threw her bitter letter into the wastebasket, and thanked Almighty God that I wasn't married to her. Her letter didn't tell me anything at all about General Booth, but it did tell me a lot about her. Schopenhauer had said it years ago: "Vulgar people take huge delight in the faults and follies of great men."

One hardly thinks of the president of Yale as a vulgar man; yet a former president of Yale, Timothy Dwight, apparently took huge delight in denouncing a man who was running for President of the United States. The president of Yale warned that if this man were elected President, "we may see our wives and daughters the victims of legal prostitution, soberly dishonored, speciously polluted; the outcasts of delicacy and virtue, the loathing of God and man."

Sounds almost like a denunciation of Hitler, doesn't it? But it wasn't. It was a denunciation of Thomas Jefferson. *Which* Thomas Jefferson? Surely not the *immortal* Thomas

Jefferson, the author of the Declaration of Independence, the patron saint of democracy? Yea, verily, that was the man.

What American do you suppose was denounced as a "hypocrite," "an impostor," and as "little better than a murderer"? A newspaper cartoon depicted him on a guillotine, the big knife ready to cut off his head. Crowds jeered at him and hissed him as he rode through the streets. Who was he? George Washington.

But that occurred a long time ago. Maybe human nature has improved since then. Let's see. Let's take the case of Admiral Peary—the explorer who startled and thrilled the world by reaching the North Pole with dog sleds on April 6, 1909—a goal that brave men for centuries had suffered and starved and died to attain. Peary himself almost died from cold and starvation; and eight of his toes were frozen so hard they had to be cut off. He was so overwhelmed with disasters that he feared he would go insane. His superior naval officers in Washington were burned up because Peary was getting so much publicity and acclaim. So they accused him of collecting money for scientific expeditions and then "lying around and loafing in the Arctic." And they probably believed it, because it is almost impossible not to believe what you want to believe. Their determination to humiliate and block Peary was so violent that only a direct order from President McKinley enabled Peary to continue his career in the Arctic.

Would Peary have been denounced if he had had a desk job in the Navy Department in Washington? No. He wouldn't have been important enough then to have aroused jealousy.

General Grant had an even worse experience than Admiral Peary. In 1862, General Grant won the first great decisive victory that the North had enjoyed—a victory that was achieved in one afternoon, a victory that made Grant a national idol overnight—a victory that had tremendous repercussions even in far-off Europe—a victory that set church bells ringing and bonfires blazing from Maine to the banks of the Mississippi. Yet within six weeks after achieving that great victory, Grant—hero of the North—was *arrested and his army was taken from him. He wept with humiliation and despair.*

Why was General U. S. Grant arrested at the flood tide of his victory? Largely because he had aroused the jealousy and envy of his arrogant superiors.

If we are tempted to be worried about unjust criticism, here is a vital rule:

Remember that unjust criticism is often a disguised compliment. Remember that no one ever kicks a dead dog.

Chapter 7

DO THIS—AND CRITICISM CAN'T HURT YOU

I once interviewed Major General Smedley Butler—old "Gimlet-Eye." Old "Hell-Devil" Butler! Remember him? The most colorful, swashbuckling general who ever commanded the United States Marines.

He told me that when he was young, he was desperately eager to be popular, wanted to make a good impression on everyone. In those days the slightest criticism smarted and stung. But he confessed that thirty years in the Marines had toughened his hide. "I have been berated and insulted," he said, "and denounced as a yellow dog, a snake, and a skunk. I have been cursed by the experts. I have been called every possible combination of unprintable cuss words in the English language. Bother me? Huh! When I hear somebody cussing me now, I never turn my head to see who is talking."

Maybe old "Gimlet-Eye" Butler was too indifferent to criticism; but one thing is sure: most of us take the little jibes and javelins that are hurled at us far too seriously. I remember the time, years ago, when a reporter from the New York *Sun* attended a demonstration meeting of my adult-education classes and lampooned me and my work. Was I burned up? I took it as a personal insult. I telephoned Gil Hodges, the Chairman of the Executive Committee of the *Sun,* and practically demanded that he print an article stating the facts—instead of ridicule. I was determined to make the punishment fit the crime.

I am ashamed now of the way I acted. I realize now that half the people who bought the paper never saw that article. Half of those who read it regarded it as a source of innocent merriment. Half of those who gloated over it forgot all about it in a few weeks.

52

I realize now that people are not thinking about you and me or caring what is said about us. They are thinking about themselves—before breakfast, after breakfast, and right on until ten minutes past midnight. They would be a thousand times more concerned about a slight headache of their own than they would about the news of your death or mine.

Even if you and I are lied about, ridiculed, double-crossed, knifed in the back, and sold down the river by one out of every six of our most intimate friends—let's not indulge in an orgy of self-pity. Instead, let's remind ourselves that that's precisely what happened to Jesus. One of His twelve most intimate friends turned traitor for a bribe that would amount, in our modern money, to about nineteen dollars. Another one of His twelve most intimate friends openly deserted Jesus the moment He got into trouble, and declared three times that he didn't even know Jesus—and he swore as he said it. One out of six! That is what happened to Jesus. Why should you and I expect a better score?

I discovered years ago that although I couldn't keep people from criticizing me unjustly, I could do something infinitely more important: I could determine whether I would let the unjust condemnation disturb me.

Let's be clear about this: I am not advocating ignoring all criticism. Far from it. I am talking about *ignoring only unjust criticism.* I once asked Eleanor Roosevelt how she handled unjust criticism—and Allah knows she had a lot of it. She probably had more ardent friends and more violent enemies than any other woman who ever lived in the White House.

She told me that as a young girl she was almost morbidly shy, afraid of what people might say. She was so afraid of criticism that one day she asked her aunt, Theodore Roosevelt's sister, for advice. She said: "Auntie Bye, I want to do so-and-so. But I'm afraid of being criticized."

Teddy Roosevelt's sister looked her in the eye and said: "Never be bothered by what people say, as long as you know in your heart you are right." Eleanor Roosevelt told me that that bit of advice proved to be her Rock of Gibraltar years later, when she was in the White House. She told me that the only way we can avoid all criticism is to be like a Dresden-china figure and stay on a shelf. "Do what you feel in your heart to be right—for you'll be criticized, anyway. You'll be 'damned if you do, and damned if you don't.' " That is her advice.

When the late Matthew C. Brush was president of the American International Corporation at 40 Wall Street, I asked him if he was ever sensitive to criticism; and he replied, "Yes, I was very sensitive to it in my early days. I was eager then to have all the employees in the organization think I was perfect. If they didn't, it worried me. I would try to please first one person who had been sounding off against me; but the very thing I did to patch it up with him would make someone else mad. Then when I tried to fix it up with this person, I would stir up a couple of other bumblebees. I finally discovered that the more I tried to pacify and to smooth over injured feelings in order to escape personal criticism, the more certain I was to increase my enemies. So finally I said to myself, 'If you get your head above the crowd, you're going to be criticized. So get used to the idea.' That helped me tremendously. From that time on I made it a rule to do the very best I could and then put up my old umbrella and let the rain of criticism drain off me instead of run down my neck."

Deems Taylor went a bit further: he let the rain of criticism run down his neck and had a good laugh over it—in public. When he was giving his comments during the intermission of the Sunday-afternoon radio concerts of the New York Philharmonic Symphony Orchestra, one woman wrote him a letter calling him "a liar, a traitor, a snake, and a moron." Mr. Taylor says in his book, *Of Men and Music:* "I have a suspicion that she didn't care for that talk." On the following week's broadcast, Mr. Taylor read this letter over the radio to millions of listeners—and received another letter from the same lady a few days later, "expressing her unaltered opinion," says Mr. Taylor, "that I was *still* a liar, a traitor, a snake, and a moron." We can't keep from admiring a man who takes criticism like that. We admire his serenity, his unshaken poise, and his sense of humor.

When Charles Schwab was addressing the student body at Princeton, he confessed that one of the most important lessons he had ever learned was taught to him by an old German who worked in Schwab's steel mill. This old German got involved in a hot wartime argument with the other steelworkers, and they tossed him into the river. "When he came into my office," Mr. Schwab said, "covered with mud and water, I asked him what he had said to the men who had thrown him into the river, and he replied: 'I yust laughed.'"

Mr. Schwab declared that he had adopted that old German's words as his motto: "Yust laugh."

That motto is especially good when you are the victim of unjust criticism. You can answer the man who answers you back, but what can you say to the man who "yust laughs"?

Lincoln might have broken under the strain of the Civil War if he hadn't learned the folly of trying to answer all the vitriolic condemnations hurled at him. His description of how he handled his critics has become a literary gem—a classic. General MacArthur had a copy of it hanging above his headquarters desk during the war; and Winston Churchill had a framed copy of it on the walls of his study at Chartwell. It goes like this: "If I were to try to read, much less to answer, all the attacks made on me, this shop might as well be closed for any other business. I do the very best I know how—the very best I can; and I mean to keep on doing so until the end. If the end brings me out all right, then what is said against me won't matter. If the end brings me out wrong, then ten angels swearing I was right would make no difference."

When you and I are unjustly criticized, let's remember the rule:

Do the very best you can; and then put up your old umbrella and keep the rain of criticism from running down the back of your neck.

Part Two

Fundamental Techniques in Handling People

How to Win Friends and Influence People is a book on human relations—on getting along with people, on the need for friends in living a full life. Resisting the temptation to criticize and getting in the habit of giving praise and honest appreciation will do more than anything else to make people like us. And the same things that make us happy in the world will give us a happy home life too—the first need of every man and woman.

Chapter 8

"IF YOU WANT TO GATHER HONEY,
DON'T KICK OVER THE BEEHIVE"

On May 7, 1931, New York City witnessed the most sensational man-hunt the old town had ever known. After weeks of search, "Two Gun" Crowley—the killer, the gunman who didn't smoke or drink—was at bay, trapped in his sweetheart's apartment on West End Avenue.

One hundred and fifty policemen and detectives laid siege to his top-floor hideaway. Chopping holes in the roof, they tried to smoke out Crowley, the "cop killer," with tear gas. Then they mounted their machine guns on surrounding buildings, and for more than an hour one of New York's fine residential sections reverberated with the crack of pistol fire and the rat-tat-tat of machine guns. Crowley, crouching behind an overstuffed chair, fired incessantly at the police. Ten thousand excited people watched the battle. Nothing like it had ever been seen before on the sidewalks of New York.

When Crowley was captured, Police Commissioner Mulrooney declared that the two-gun desperado was one of the most dangerous criminals ever encountered in the history of New York. "He will kill," said the Commissioner, "at the drop of a feather."

But how did "Two Gun" Crowley regard himself? We know, because while the police were firing into his apartment, he wrote a letter addressed "To whom it may concern." And, as he wrote, the blood flowing from his wounds left a crimson trail on the paper. In this letter Crowley said: "Under my coat is a weary heart, but a kind one—one that would do nobody any harm."

A short time before this, Crowley had been having a necking party on a country road out on Long Island. Suddenly a policeman walked up to the parked car and said: "Let me see your license."

Without saying a word, Crowley drew his gun, and cut the policeman down with a shower of lead. As the dying officer fell, Crowley leaped out of the car, grabbed the officer's revolver, and fired another bullet into the prostrate body. And that was the killer who said: "Under my coat is a weary heart, but a kind one—one that would do nobody any harm."

Crowley was sentenced to the electric chair. When he arrived at the death house at Sing Sing, did he say, "This is what I get for killing people?" No, he said: "This is what I get for defending myself."

The point of the story is this: "Two Gun" Crowley didn't blame himself for anything.

Is that an unusual attitude among criminals? If you think so, listen to this:

"I have spent the best years of my life giving people the lighter pleasures, helping them have a good time, and all I get is abuse, the existence of a hunted man."

That's Al Capone speaking. Yes, America's erstwhile Public Enemy Number One—the most sinister gang leader who ever shot up Chicago. Capone doesn't condemn himself. He actually regards himself as a public benefactor—an unappreciated and misunderstood public benefactor.

And so did Dutch Schultz before he crumpled up under gangster bullets in Newark. Dutch Schultz, one of New York's most notorious rats, said in a newspaper interview that he was a public benefactor. And he believed it.

I have had some interesting correspondence with Warden Lawes of Sing Sing on this subject, and he declares that "few of the criminals in Sing Sing regard themselves as bad men. They are just as human as you and I. So they rationalize, they explain. They can tell you why they had to crack a safe or be quick on the trigger finger. Most of them attempt by a form of reasoning, fallacious or logical, to justify their anti-social acts even to themselves, consequently stoutly maintaining that they should never have been imprisoned at all."

If Al Capone, "Two Gun" Crowley, Dutch Schultz, the desperate men behind prison walls don't blame themselves for anything—what about the people with whom you and I come in contact?

The late John Wanamaker once confessed: "I learned thirty years ago that it is foolish to scold. I have enough trouble overcoming my own limitations without fretting over the fact that God has not seen fit to distribute evenly the gift of intelligence."

Wanamaker learned this lesson early; but I personally had to blunder through this old world for a third of a century before it even began to dawn upon me that ninety-nine times out of a hundred, no man ever criticizes himself for anything, no matter how wrong he may be.

Criticism is futile because it puts a man on the defensive, and usually makes him strive to justify himself. Criticism is dangerous, because it wounds a man's precious pride, hurts his sense of importance, and arouses his resentment.

The German army won't let a soldier file a complaint and make a criticism immediately after a thing has happened. He has to sleep on his grudge first and cool off. If he files his complaint immediately, he is punished. By the eternals, there ought to be a law like that in civil life too—a law for whining parents and nagging wives and scolding employers and the whole obnoxious parade of fault-finders.

You will find examples of the futility of criticism bristling on a thousand pages of history. Take, for example, the famous quarrel between Theodore Roosevelt and President Taft—a quarrel that split the Republican Party, put Woodrow Wilson in the White House, and wrote bold, luminous lines across the World War and altered the flow of history. Let's review the facts quickly: When Theodore Roosevelt stepped out of the White House in 1908, he made Taft president, and then went off to Africa to shoot lions. When he returned, he exploded. He denounced Taft for his conservatism, tried to secure the nomination for a third term himself, formed the Bull Moose Party, and all but demolished the G.O.P. In the

election that followed, William Howard Taft and the
Republican Party carried only two states—Vermont and
Utah. The most disastrous defeat the old party had ever
known.

Theodore Roosevelt blamed Taft; but did President
Taft blame himself? Of course not. With tears in his eyes,
Taft said: "I don't see how I could have done any dif-
ferently from what I have."

Who was to blame? Roosevelt or Taft? Frankly, I
don't know, and I don't care. The point I am trying to
make is that all of Theodore Roosevelt's criticism didn't
persuade Taft that he was wrong. It merely made Taft
strive to justify himself and to reiterate with tears in his
eyes: "I don't see how I could have done any differently
from what I have."

Or, take the Teapot Dome Oil scandal. Remember it?
It kept the newspapers ringing with indignation for years.
It rocked the nation! Nothing like it had ever happened
before in American public life within the memory of
living men. Here are the bare facts of the scandal: Albert
Fall, Secretary of the Interior in Harding's cabinet, was
entrusted with the leasing of government oil reserves at
Elk Hill and Teapot Dome—oil reserves that had been
set aside for the future use of the Navy. Did Secretary
Fall permit competitive bidding? No sir. He handed the
fat, juicy contract outright to his friend, Edward L. Doheny. And what did Doheny do? He gave Secretary Fall
what he was pleased to call a "loan" of one hundred thousand dollars. Then, in a high-handed manner, Secretary
Fall ordered United States Marines into the district to
drive off competitors whose adjacent wells were sapping
oil out of the Elk Hill reserves. These competitors, driven
off their ground at the ends of guns and bayonets, rushed
into court—and blew the lid off the hundred-million-
dollar Teapot Dome scandal. A stench arose so vile that
it ruined the Harding administration, nauseated an entire
nation, threatened to wreck the Republican Party, and put
Albert B. Fall behind prison bars.

Fall was condemned viciously—condemned as few
men in public life have ever been. Did he repent? Never!

Years later Herbert Hoover intimated in a public speech that President Harding's death had been due to mental anxiety and worry because a friend had betrayed him. When Mrs. Fall heard that, she sprang from her chair, she wept, she shook her fists at fate, and screamed: "What! Harding betrayed by Fall? No! My husband never betrayed anyone. This whole house full of gold would not tempt my husband to do wrong. He is the one who has been betrayed and led to the slaughter and crucified."

There you are; human nature in action, the wrongdoer blaming everybody but himself. We are all like that. So when you and I are tempted to criticize someone tomorrow, let's remember Al Capone, "Two Gun" Crowley, and Albert Fall. Let's realize that criticisms are like homing pigeons. They always return home. Let's realize that the person we are going to correct and condemn will probably justify himself, and condemn us in return; or, like the gentle Taft, he will say: "I don't see how I could have done any differently from what I have."

On Saturday morning, April 15, 1865, Abraham Lincoln lay dying in a hall bedroom of a cheap lodging house directly across the street from Ford's Theatre, where Booth had shot him. Lincoln's long body lay stretched diagonally across a sagging bed that was too short for him. A cheap reproduction of Rosa Bonheur's famous painting, "The Horse Fair," hung above the bed, and a dismal gas jet flickered yellow light.

As Lincoln lay dying, Secretary of War Stanton said, "There lies the most perfect ruler of men that the world has ever seen."

What was the secret of Lincoln's success in dealing with men? I studied the life of Abraham Lincoln for ten years, and devoted all of three years to writing and rewriting a book entitled *Lincoln the Unknown.* I believe I have made as detailed and exhaustive a study of Lincoln's personality and home life as it is possible for any human being to make. I made a special study of Lincoln's method of dealing with men. Did he indulge in criticism? Oh, yes. As a young man in the Pigeon Creek Valley of

Indiana, he not only criticized but he wrote letters and poems ridiculing people and dropped these letters on the country roads where they were sure to be found. One of these letters aroused resentments that burned for a lifetime.

Even after Lincoln had become a practicing lawyer in Springfield, Illinois, he attacked his opponents openly in letters published in the newspapers. But he did this just once too often.

In the autumn of 1842, he ridiculed a vain, pugnacious Irish politician by the name of James Shields. Lincoln lampooned him through an anonymous letter published in the *Springfield Journal*. The town roared with laughter. Shields, sensitive and proud, boiled with indignation. He found out who wrote the letter, leaped on his horse, started after Lincoln, and challenged him to fight a duel. Lincoln didn't want to fight. He was opposed to dueling; but he couldn't get out of it and save his honor. He was given the choice of weapons. Since he had very long arms, he chose cavalry broad swords, took lessons in sword fighting from a West Point graduate; and, on the appointed day, he and Shields met on a sand bar in the Mississippi River, prepared to fight to the death; but, at the last minute, their seconds interrupted and stopped the duel.

That was the most lurid personal incident in Lincoln's life. It taught him an invaluable lesson in the art of dealing with people. Never again did he write an insulting letter. Never again did he ridicule anyone. And from that time on, he almost never criticized anybody for anything.

Time after time, during the Civil War, Lincoln put a new general at the head of the Army of the Potomac, and each one in turn—McClellan, Pope, Burnside, Hooker, Meade—blundered tragically, and drove Lincoln to pacing the floor in despair. Half the nation savagely condemned these incompetent generals, but Lincoln, "with malice towards none, with charity for all," held his peace. One of his favorite quotations was, "Judge not, that ye be not judged."

And when Mrs. Lincoln and others spoke harshly of the Southern people, Lincoln replied: "Don't criticize them; they are just what we would be under similar circumstances."

Yet, if any man ever had occasion to criticize, surely it was Lincoln. Let's take just one illustration:

The Battle of Gettysburg was fought during the first three days of July, 1863. During the night of July 4, Lee began to retreat southward while storm clouds deluged the country with rain. When Lee reached the Potomac with his defeated army, he found a swollen, impassable river in front of him, and a victorious Union army behind him. Lee was in a trap. He couldn't escape. Lincoln saw that. Here was a golden, heaven-sent opportunity—the opportunity to capture Lee's army and end the war immediately. So, with a surge of high hope, Lincoln ordered Meade not to call a council of war but to attack Lee immediately. Lincoln telegraphed his orders and then sent a special messenger to Meade demanding immediate action.

And what did General Meade do? He did the very opposite of what he was told to do. He called a council of war in direct violation of Lincoln's orders. He hesitated. He procrastinated. He telegraphed all manner of excuses. He refused point blank to attack Lee. Finally the waters receded and Lee escaped over the Potomac with his forces.

Lincoln was furious. "What does this mean?" Lincoln cried to his son Robert. "Great God! What does this mean? We had them within our grasp, and had only to stretch forth our hands and they were ours; yet nothing that I could say or do could make the army move. Under the circumstances, almost any general could have defeated Lee. If I had gone up there, I could have whipped him myself."

In bitter disappointment, Lincoln sat down and wrote Meade this letter. And remember, at this period of his life he was extremely conservative and restrained in his phraseology. So this letter coming from Lincoln in 1863 was tantamount to the severest rebuke.

"My dear General,

"I do not believe you appreciate the magnitude of the misfortune involved in Lee's escape. He was within our easy grasp, and to have closed upon him would, in connection with our other late successes, have ended the war. As it is, the war will be prolonged indefinitely. If you could not safely attack Lee last Monday, how can you possibly do so south of the river, when you can take with you very few— no more than two-thirds of the force you then had in hand? It would be unreasonable to expect and I do not expect that you can now effect much. Your golden opportunity is gone, and I am distressed immeasurably because of it."

What do you suppose Meade did when he read that letter?

Meade never saw that letter. Lincoln never mailed it. It was found among Lincoln's papers after his death.

My guess is—and this is only a guess—that after writing that letter, Lincoln looked out of the window and said to himself, "Just a minute. Maybe I ought not to be so hasty. It is easy enough for me to sit there in the quiet of the White House and order Meade to attack; but if I had been up at Gettysburg, and if I had seen as much blood as Meade has seen during the last week, and if my ears had been pierced with the screams and shrieks of the wounded and dying, maybe I wouldn't be so anxious to attack either. If I had Meade's timid temperament, perhaps I would have done just what he has done. Anyhow, it is water under the bridge now. If I send this letter, it will relieve my feelings but it will make Meade try to justify himself. It will make him condemn me. It will arouse hard feelings, impair all his further usefulness as a commander, and perhaps force him to resign from the army."

So, as I have already said, Lincoln put the letter aside, for he had learned by bitter experience that sharp criticisms and rebukes almost invariably end in futility.

Theodore Roosevelt said that when he, as President,

was confronted with some perplexing problem, he used to lean back and look up at a large painting of Lincoln that hung above his desk in the White House and ask himself, "What would Lincoln do if he were in my shoes? How would he solve this problem?"

The next time we are tempted to give somebody "hail Columbia," let's pull a five-dollar bill out of our pocket, look at Lincoln's picture on the bill, and ask, "How would Lincoln handle this problem if he had it?"

Do you know someone you would like to change and regulate and improve? Good! That is fine. I am all in favor of it. But why not begin on yourself? From a purely selfish standpoint, that is a lot more profitable than trying to improve others—yes, and a lot less dangerous.

"When a man's fight begins with himself," said Browning, "he is worth something." It will probably take from now until Christmas to perfect yourself. You can then have a nice long rest over the holidays and devote the New Year to regulating and criticizing other people.

But perfect yourself first.

"Don't complain about the snow on your neighbor's roof," said Confucius, "when your own doorstep is unclean."

When I was still young and trying hard to impress people, I wrote a foolish letter to Richard Harding Davis, an author who once loomed large on the literary horizon of America. I was preparing a magazine article about authors; and I asked Davis to tell me about his method of work. A few weeks earlier, I had received a letter from someone with this notation at the bottom: "Dictated but not read." I was quite impressed. I felt the writer must be very big and busy and important. I wasn't the slightest bit busy; but I was eager to make an impression on Richard Harding Davis so I ended my short note with the words: "Dictated but not read."

He never troubled to answer the letter. He simply returned it to me with this scribbled across the bottom:

"Your bad manners are exceeded only by your bad manners." True, I had blundered, and perhaps I deserved his rebuke. But, being human, I resented it. I resented it so sharply that when I read of the death of Richard Harding Davis ten years later, the one thought that still persisted in my mind—I am ashamed to admit—was the hurt he had given me.

If you and I want to stir up a resentment tomorrow that may rankle across the decades and endure until death, just let us indulge in a little stinging criticism—no matter how certain we are that it is justified.

When dealing with people, let us remember we are not dealing with creatures of logic. We are dealing with creatures of emotion, creatures bristling with prejudices and motivated by pride and vanity.

And criticism is a dangerous spark—a spark that is liable to cause an explosion in the powder magazine of pride—an explosion that sometimes hastens death. For example, General Leonard Wood was criticized and not allowed to go with the army to France. That blow to his pride probably shortened his life.

Bitter criticism caused the sensitive Thomas Hardy, one of the finest novelists that ever enriched English literature, to give up the writing of fiction forever. Criticism drove Thomas Chatterton, the English poet, to suicide.

Benjamin Franklin, tactless in his youth, became so diplomatic, so adroit at handling people that he was made American Ambassador to France. The secret of his success? "I will speak ill of no man," he said, ". . . and speak all the good I know of everybody."

Any fool can criticize, condemn, and complain—and most fools do.

But it takes character and self-control to be understanding and forgiving.

"A great man shows his greatness," said Carlyle, "by the way he treats little men."

Instead of condemning people, let's try to understand them. Let's try to figure out why they do what they do. That's a lot more profitable and intriguing than criticism;

and it breeds sympathy, tolerance, and kindness. "To know all is to forgive all."

As Dr. Johnson said: "God Himself, sir, does not propose to judge man until the end of his days."

Why should you and I?

Chapter 9

THE BIG SECRET OF DEALING WITH PEOPLE

There is only one way under high Heaven to get anybody to do anything. Did you ever stop to think of that?
Yes, just one way. And that is by making the other person
want to do it.

Remember, there is no other way.

Of course, you can make a man want to give you his
watch by sticking a revolver in his ribs. You can make
an employee give you co-operation—until your back is
turned—by threatening to fire him. You can make a
child do what you want it to do by a whip or a threat.
But these crude methods have sharply undesirable repercussions.

The only way I can get you to do anything is by
giving you what you want.

What do you want?

The famous Dr. Sigmund Freud of Vienna, one of the
most distinguished psychologists of the twentieth century,
said that everything you and I do springs from two motives: the sex urge and the desire to be great.

Professor John Dewey, America's most profound phi-
losopher, phrased it a bit differently. Dr. Dewey said the
deepest urge in human nature is "the desire to be important." Remember that phrase: "the desire to be important." It is significant. You are going to hear a lot
about it in this book.

What do you want? Not many things, but the few
things that you do wish, you crave with an insistence
that will not be denied. Almost every normal adult
wants—

1. Health and the preservation of life.
2. Food.
3. Sleep.
4. Money and the things money will buy.
5. Life in the hereafter.
6. Sexual gratification.
7. The well-being of our children.
8. A feeling of importance.

Almost all these wants are gratified—all except one. But there is one longing almost as deep, almost as imperious, as the desire for food or sleep which is seldom gratified. It is what Freud calls "the desire to be great." It is what Dewey calls the "desire to be important."

Lincoln once began a letter by saying: "Everybody likes a compliment." William James said: "The deepest principle in human nature is the craving to be appreciated." He didn't speak, mind you, of the "wish" or the "desire" or the "longing" to be appreciated. He said the *"craving"* to be appreciated.

Here is a gnawing and unfaltering human hunger; and the rare individual who honestly satisfies this heart-hunger will hold people in the palm of his hand and "even the undertaker will be sorry when he dies."

The desire for a feeling of importance is one of the chief distinguishing differences between mankind and the animals. To illustrate: When I was a farm boy out in Missouri, my father bred fine Duroc-Jersey hogs and pedigreed white-faced cattle. We used to exhibit our hogs and white-faced cattle at the country fairs and livestock shows throughout the Middle West. We won first prizes by the score. My father pinned his blue ribbons on a sheet of white muslin, and when friends or visitors came to the house, he would get out the long sheet of muslin. He would hold one end and I would hold the other while he exhibited the blue ribbons.

The hogs didn't care about the ribbons they had won. But Father did. These prizes gave him a feeling of importance.

If our ancestors hadn't had this flaming urge for a

feeling of importance, civilization would have been impossible. Without it, we should have been just about like the animals.

It was this desire for a feeling of importance that led an uneducated, poverty-stricken grocery clerk to study some law books that he found in the bottom of a barrel of household plunder that he had bought for fifty cents. You have probably heard of this grocery clerk. His name was Lincoln.

It was this desire for a feeling of importance that inspired Dickens to write his immortal novels. This desire inspired Sir Christopher Wren to design his symphonies in stone. This desire made Rockefeller amass millions that he never spent! And this same desire made the richest man in your town build a house far too large for his requirements.

This desire makes you want to wear the latest styles, drive the latest car, and talk about your brilliant children.

It is this desire which lures many boys into becoming gangsters and gunmen. "The average young criminal of today," says E. P. Mulrooney, former Police Commissioner of New York, "is filled with ego, and his first request after arrest is for those lurid newspapers that make him out a hero. The disagreeable prospect of taking a 'hot squat' in the electric chair seems remote, so long as he can gloat over his likeness sharing space with pictures of Babe Ruth, LaGuardia, Einstein, Lindbergh, Toscanini, or Roosevelt."

If you tell me how you get your feelings of importance, I'll tell you what you are. That determines your character. That is the most significant thing about you. For example, John D. Rockefeller got his feeling of importance by giving money to erect a modern hospital in Peking, China, to care for millions of poor people whom he had never seen and never would see. Dillinger, on the other hand, got his feeling of importance by being a bandit, a bank robber and killer. When the G-men were hunting him, he dashed into a farmhouse up in Minnesota and said, "I'm Dillinger!" He was proud of the fact that he was Public Enemy Number One. "I'm not going to hurt you, but I'm Dillinger!" he said.

Yes, the one significant difference between Dillinger and Rockefeller is how they got their feeling of importance.

History sparkles with amusing examples of famous people struggling for a feeling of importance. Even George Washington wanted to be called "His Mightiness, the President of the United States"; and Columbus pleaded for the title, "Admiral of the Ocean and Viceroy of India." Catherine the Great refused to open letters that were not addressed to "Her Imperial Majesty"; and Mrs. Lincoln, in the White House, turned upon Mrs. Grant like a tigress and shouted, "How dare you be seated in my presence until I invite you!"

Our millionaires helped finance Admiral Byrd's expedition to the Antarctic with the understanding that ranges of icy mountains would be named after them; and Victor Hugo aspired to have nothing less than the city of Paris renamed in his honor. Even Shakespeare, mightiest of the mighty, tried to add luster to his name by procuring a coat of arms for his family.

People sometimes become invalids in order to win sympathy and attention, and get a feeling of importance. For example, take Mrs. McKinley. She got a feeling of importance by forcing her husband, the President of the United States, to neglect important affairs of state while he reclined on the bed beside her for hours at a time, his arm about her, soothing her to sleep. She fed her gnawing desire for attention by insisting that he remain with her while she was having her teeth fixed, and once created a stormy scene when he had to leave her alone with the dentist while he kept an appointment with John Hay.

Mary Roberts Rinehart once told me of a bright, vigorous young woman who became an invalid in order to get a feeling of importance. "One day," said Mrs. Rinehart, "this woman had been obliged to face something, her age perhaps, and the fact that she would never be married.

The lonely years were stretching ahead and there was little left for her to anticipate.

"She took to her bed; and for ten years her old mother traveled to the third floor and back, carrying trays, nursing her. Then one day the old mother, weary with service, lay down and died. For some weeks, the invalid languished; then she got up, put on her clothing, and resumed living again."

Some authorities declare that people may actually go insane in order to find, in the dreamland of insanity, the feeling of importance that has been denied them in the harsh world of reality. There are more patients suffering from mental diseases in the hospitals in the United States than from all other diseases combined. If you are over fifteen years of age and residing in New York State, the chances are one out of twenty that you will be confined to an insane asylum for seven years of your life.

What is the cause of insanity?

Nobody can answer such a sweeping question as that, but we know that certain diseases, such as syphilis, break down and destroy the brain cells and result in insanity. In fact, about one half of all mental diseases can be attributed to such physical causes as brain lesions, alcohol, toxins, and injuries. But the other half—and this is the appalling part of the story—the other half of the people who go insane apparently have nothing organically wrong with their brain cells. In postmortem examinations, when their brain tissues are studied under the highest-powered microscopes, they are found to be apparently just as healthy as yours and mine.

Why do these people go insane?

I recently put that question to the head physician of one of our most important hospitals for the insane. This doctor, who has received the highest honors and the most coveted awards for his knowledge of insanity, told me frankly that he didn't know why people went insane. Nobody knows for sure. But he did say that many people who go insane find in insanity a feeling of importance that they were unable to achieve in the world of reality. Then he told me this story:

"I have a patient right now whose marriage proved to be a tragedy. She wanted love, sexual gratification, children, and social prestige; but life blasted all her hopes. Her husband didn't love her. He refused even to eat with her, and forced her to serve his meals in his room upstairs. She had no children, no social standing. She went insane; and, in her imagination, she divorced her husband and resumed her maiden name. She now believes she has married into the English aristocracy, and she insists on being called Lady Smith.

"And as for children, she imagines now that she has a new child every night. Each time I call on her she says: 'Doctor, I had a baby last night.' "

Life once wrecked all her dream ships on the sharp rocks of reality; but in the sunny, fantastic isles of insanity, all her barkentines race into port with canvas billowing and with winds singing through the masts.

Tragic? Oh, I don't know. Her physician said to me: "If I could stretch out my hand and restore her sanity, I wouldn't do it. She's much happier as she is."

As a group, insane people are happier than you and I. Many enjoy being insane. Why shouldn't they? They have solved their problems. They will write you a check for a million dollars, or give you a letter of introduction to the Aga Khan. They have found in a dream world of their own creation the feeling of importance which they so deeply desired.

If some people are so hungry for a feeling of importance that they actually go insane to get it, imagine what miracles you and I can achieve by giving people honest appreciation this side of insanity.

There have been, so far as I know, only two people in history who were paid a salary of a million dollars a year: Walter Chrysler and Charles Schwab.

Why did Andrew Carnegie pay Schwab a million dollars a year, or more than three thousand dollars a day? Why?

Andrew Carnegie paid Charles Schwab a million dollars a year. Because Schwab was a genius? No. Because he knew more about the manufacture of steel than other people? Nonsense. Charles Schwab told me himself that he had many men working for him who knew more about the manufacture of steel than he did.

Schwab said that he was paid this salary largely because of his ability to deal with people. I asked him how he did it. Here is his secret set down in his own words— words that ought to be cast in eternal bronze and hung in every home and school, every shop and office in the land —words that children ought to memorize instead of wasting their time memorizing the conjugation of Latin verbs or the amount of the annual rainfall in Brazil—words that will all but transform your life and mine if we will only live them:

> *"I consider my ability to arouse enthusiasm among the men," said Schwab, "the greatest asset I possess, and the way to develop the best that is in a man is by appreciation and encouragement.*
> *"There is nothing else that so kills the ambitions of a man as criticisms from his superiors. I never criticize anyone. I believe in giving a man incentive to work. So I am anxious to praise but loath to find fault. If I like anything, I am hearty in my approbation and lavish in my praise."*

That is what Schwab did. But what does the average man do? The exact opposite. If he doesn't like a thing, he raises the Old Harry; if he does like it, he says nothing.

"In my wide association in life, meeting with many and great men in various parts of the world," Schwab declared, "I have yet to find the man, however great or exalted his station, who did not do better work and put forth greater effort under a spirit of approval than he would ever do under a spirit of criticism."

That, he said frankly, was one of the outstanding reasons for the phenomenal success of Andrew Carnegie. Carnegie praised his associates publicly as well as privately.

Carnegie wanted to praise his assistants even on his tombstone. He wrote an epitaph for himself which read: "Here lies one who knew how to get around him men who were cleverer than himself."

Sincere appreciation was one of the secrets of Rockefeller's success in handling men. For example, when one of his partners, Edward T. Bedford, pulled a boner and lost the firm a million dollars by a bad buy in South America, John D. might have criticized; but he knew Bedford had done his best—and the incident was closed. So Rockefeller found something to praise; he congratulated Bedford because he had been able to save sixty per cent of the money he had invested. "That's splendid," said Rockefeller. "We don't always do as well as that upstairs."

Ziegfeld, the most spectacular *entrepreneur* who ever dazzled Broadway, gained his reputation by his subtle ability to "glorify the American girl." He repeatedly took some drab little creature that no one ever looked at twice and transformed her on the stage into a glamorous vision of mystery and seduction. Knowing the value of appreciation and confidence, he made women *feel* beautiful by the sheer power of his gallantry and consideration. He was practical: he raised the salary of chorus girls from thirty dollars a week to as high as one hundred and seventy-five. And he was also chivalrous: on opening night at the Follies, he sent a telegram to the stars in the cast, and he deluged every chorus girl in the show with American Beauty roses.

I once succumbed to the fad of fasting and went for six days and nights without eating. It wasn't difficult. I was less hungry at the end of the sixth day than I was at the end of the second. Yet I know, and you know, people who would think they had committed a crime if they let their families or employees go for six days without food; but they will let them go for six days, and six weeks, and sometimes sixty years without giving them the hearty appreciation that they crave almost as much as they crave food.

When Alfred Lunt played the stellar role in *Reunion in Vienna,* he said, "There is nothing I need so much as nourishment for my self-esteem."

We nourish the bodies of our children and friends and employees; but how seldom do we nourish their self-esteem. We provide them with roast beef and potatoes to build energy; but we neglect to give them kind words of appreciation that would sing in their memories for years like the music of the morning stars.

Some readers are saying right now as they read these lines: "Old stuff! Soft soap! Bear oil! Flattery! I've tried that stuff. It doesn't work—not with intelligent people."

Of course, flattery seldom works with discerning people. It is shallow, selfish, and insincere. It ought to fail and it usually does. True, some people are so hungry, so thirsty, for appreciation that they will swallow anything, just as a starving man will eat grass and fish worms.

Why, for example, were the much-married Mdivani brothers such flaming successes in the matrimonial market? Why were these so-called "Princes" able to marry two beautiful and famous screen stars and a world-famous prima donna and Barbara Hutton with her five-and-ten-cent-store millions? Why? How did they do it?

"The Mdivani charm for women," said Adela Rogers St. Johns, in an article in the magazine *Liberty,* ". . . has been among the mysteries of the ages to many.

"Pola Negri, a woman of the world, a connoisseur of men, and a great artist, once explained it to me. She said, 'They understand the art of flattery as do no other men I have ever met. And the art of flattery is almost a lost one in this realistic and humorous age. That, I assure you, is the secret of the Mdivani charm for women. I know.'"

Even Queen Victoria was susceptible to flattery. Disraeli confessed that he put it on thick in dealing with the Queen. To use his exact words, he said he "spread it on with a trowel." But Disraeli was one of the most polished, deft, and adroit men who ever ruled the far-flung British Empire. He was a genius in his line. What would work for him wouldn't necessarily work for you and me. In the long run, flattery will do you more harm than good. Flattery is counterfeit, and like counterfeit money, it will eventually get you into trouble if you try to pass it.

The difference between appreciation and flattery? That is simple. One is sincere and the other insincere. One comes from the heart out; the other from the teeth out. One is unselfish; the other is selfish. One is universally admired; the other is universally condemned.

I recently saw a bust of General Obregon in the Chapultepec palace in Mexico City. Below the bust are carved these wise words from General Obregon's philosophy: "Don't be afraid of enemies who attack you. Be afraid of friends who flatter you."

No! No! No! I am not suggesting flattery! Far from it. I'm talking about a new way of life. Let me repeat. *I am talking about a new way of life.*

King George V had a set of six maxims displayed on the walls of his study at Buckingham Palace. One of these maxims said: "Teach me neither to proffer nor receive cheap praise." That's all flattery is: cheap praise. I once read a definition of flattery that may be worth repeating: "Flattery is telling the other man precisely what he thinks about himself."

"Use what language you will," said Ralph Waldo Emerson, "you can never say anything but what you are."

If all we had to do was to use flattery, everybody would catch on to it and we should all be experts in human relations.

When we are not engaged in thinking about some definite problem, we usually spend about 95 per cent of our time thinking about ourselves. Now, if we stop thinking about ourselves for a while and begin to think of the other man's good points, we won't have to resort to flattery so cheap and false that it can be spotted almost before it is out of the mouth.

Emerson said: "Every man I meet is my superior in some way. In that, I learn of him."

If that was true of Emerson, isn't it likely to be a thousand times more true of you and me? Let's cease thinking of our accomplishments, our wants. Let's try to figure out the other man's good points. Then forget flattery. Give honest, sincere appreciation. Be "hearty in your approbation and lavish in your praise," and people will cherish your words and treasure them and repeat them over a lifetime—repeat them years after you have forgotten them.

Chapter 10

"HE WHO CAN DO THIS HAS THE WHOLE WORLD WITH HIM. HE WHO CANNOT WALKS A LONELY WAY."

I go fishing up in Maine every summer. Personally I am very fond of strawberries and cream; but I find that for some strange reason fish prefer worms. So when I go fishing, I don't think about what I want. I think about what they want. I don't bait the hook with strawberries and cream. Rather, I dangle a worm or a grasshopper in front of the fish and say: "Wouldn't you like to have that?"

Why not use the same common sense when fishing for men?

That is what Lloyd George did. When someone asked him how he managed to stay in power after all the other wartime leaders—Wilson, Orlando, and Clemenceau—had been ousted and forgotten, he replied that if his staying on top might be attributed to any one thing, it was probably to the fact that he had learned it was necessary to bait the hook to suit the fish.

Why talk about what we want? That is childish. Absurd. Of course, you are interested in what you want. You are eternally interested in it. But no one else is. The rest of us are just like you: we are interested in what we want.

So the only way on earth to influence the other fellow is to talk about what he wants and show him how to get it.

Remember that tomorrow when you are trying to get somebody to do something. If, for example, you don't want your son to smoke, don't preach at him, and don't talk about what you want; but show him that cigarettes

81

may keep him from making the baseball team or winning the hundred-yard dash.

This is a good thing to remember regardless of whether you are dealing with children or calves or chimpanzees. For example: Ralph Waldo Emerson and his son one day tried to get a calf into the barn. But they made the common mistake of thinking only of what they wanted: Emerson pushed and his son pulled. But the calf did just what they did: he thought only of what he wanted; so he stiffened his legs and stubbornly refused to leave the pasture. The Irish housemaid saw their predicament. She couldn't write essays and books; but, on this occasion at least, she had more horse sense, or calf sense, than Emerson had. She thought of what the calf wanted; so she put her maternal finger in the calf's mouth, and let the calf suck her finger as she gently led him into the barn.

Every act you ever performed since the day you were born is because you wanted something. How about the time you gave a hundred dollars to the Red Cross? Yes, that is no exception to the rule. You gave the Red Cross a hundred dollars because you wanted to lend a helping hand; you wanted to do a beautiful, unselfish, divine act. "Inasmuch as ye have done it unto one of the least of these my brethren, ye have done it unto me."

If you hadn't wanted that feeling more than you wanted your hundred dollars, you would not have made the contribution. Of course, you may have made the contribution because you were ashamed to refuse or because a customer asked you to do it. But one thing is certain. You made the contribution because you wanted something.

Professor Harry A. Overstreet in his illuminating book, *Influencing Human Behavior,* says: "Action springs out of what we fundamentally desire . . . and the best piece of advice which can be given to would-be persuaders, whether in business, in the home, in the school, in politics, is: first, arouse in the other person an eager want. He who can do this has the whole world with him. He who cannot walks a lonely way!"

Andrew Carnegie, the poverty-stricken Scotch lad who started to work at two cents an hour and finally gave away three hundred and sixty-five million dollars—he learned early in life that the only way to influence people is to talk in terms of what the other person wants. He attended school only four years, yet he learned how to handle people.

To illustrate: His sister-in-law was worried sick over her two boys. They were at Yale, and they were so busy with their own affairs that they neglected to write home and paid no attention whatever to their mother's frantic letters.

Then Carnegie offered to wager a hundred dollars that he could get an answer by return mail, without even asking for it. Someone called his bet; so he wrote his nephews a chatty letter, mentioning casually in a post-script that he was sending each one a five-dollar bill.

He neglected, however, to enclose the money.

Back came replies by return mail thanking "Dear Uncle Andrew" for his kind note and—you can finish the sentence yourself.

Tomorrow you will want to persuade somebody to do something. Before you speak, pause and ask: "How can I make him *want* to do it?"

That question will stop us from rushing in heedlessly to see people with futile chatter about our desires.

I rent the grand ballroom of a certain New York hotel for twenty nights in each season in order to hold a series of lectures.

At the beginning of one season, I was suddenly informed that I should have to pay almost three times as much rent as formerly. This news reached me after the tickets had been printed and distributed and all announcements had been made.

Naturally, I didn't want to pay the increase, but what was the use of talking to the hotel about what I wanted? They were interested only in what they wanted. So a couple of days later I went in to see the manager.

"I was a bit shocked when I got your letter," I said, "but I don't blame you at all. If I had been in your position, I should have written a similar letter myself. Your duty as the manager of this hotel is to make all the profit possible. If you don't do that, you will be fired and you ought to be fired. Now, let's take a piece of paper and write down the advantages and the disadvantages that will accrue to you, if you insist on this increase in rent."

Then I took a letterhead and ran a line through the center and headed one column "Advantages" and the other column "Disadvantages."

I wrote down under the head of "Advantages" these words: "Ballroom free." Then I went on to say: "You will have the advantage of having the ballroom free to rent for dances and conventions. That is a big advantage, for affairs like that will pay you much more than you can get for a series of lectures. If I tie your ballroom up for twenty nights during the course of the season, it is sure to mean a loss of some very profitable business to you.

"Now, let's consider the disadvantages. First, instead of increasing your income from me, you are going to decrease it. In fact, you are going to wipe it out because I cannot pay the rent you are asking. I shall be forced to hold these lectures at some other place.

"There's another disadvantage to you also. These lectures attract crowds of educated and cultured people to your hotel. That is good advertising for you, isn't it? In fact, if you spent $5,000 advertising in the newspapers, you couldn't bring as many people to look at your hotel as I can bring by these lectures. That is worth a lot to a hotel, isn't it?"

As I talked, I wrote these two "disadvantages" under the proper heading, and handed the sheet of paper to the manager, saying: "I wish you would carefully consider both the advantages and disadvantages that are going to accrue to you and then give me your final decision."

I received a letter the next day, informing me that my rent would be increased only 50 per cent instead of 300 per cent.

Mind you, I got this reduction without saying a word about what I wanted. I talked all the time about what the other person wanted, and how he could get it.

Suppose I had done the human, natural thing: suppose I had stormed into his office and said, "What do you mean by raising my rent 300 per cent when you know the tickets have been printed and the announcements made? Three hundred per cent! Ridiculous! Absurd! I won't pay it!"

What would have happened then? An argument would have begun to steam and boil and sputter—and you know how arguments end. Even if I had convinced him that he was wrong, his pride would have made it difficult for him to back down and give in.

Here is one of the best bits of advice ever given about the fine art of human relationships. "If there is any one secret of success," said Henry Ford, "it lies in the ability to get the other person's point of view and see things from his angle as well as from your own."

That is so good, I want to repeat it: "If there is any one secret of success, it lies in the ability to get the other person's point of view and see things from his angle as well as from your own."

That is so simple, so obvious, that anyone ought to see the truth of it at a glance; yet 90 per cent of the people on this earth ignore it 90 per cent of the time.

An example? Look at the letters that come across your desk tomorrow morning, and you will find that most of them violate this high canon of common sense. Take this one, a letter written by the head of the radio department of an advertising agency with offices scattered across the continent. This letter was sent to the managers of local radio stations throughout the country. (I have set down, in parentheses, my reactions to each paragraph.)

"Mr. John Blank,
Blankville,
Indiana.

Dear Mr. Blank:
The ——— company desires to retain its position in advertising agency leadership in the radio field."

(Who cares what your company desires? I am worried about my own problems. The bank is foreclosing the mortgage on my house, the bugs are destroying the hollyhocks, the stock market tumbled yesterday, I missed the 8:15 this morning, I wasn't invited to the Jones' dance last night, the doctor tells me I have high blood pressure and neuritis and dandruff. And then what happens? I come down to the office this morning worried, open my mail, and here is some little whippersnapper off in New York yapping about what his company wants. Bah! If he only realized what sort of impression his letter makes, he would get out of the advertising business and start manufacturing sheep dip.)

"This agency's national advertising accounts were the bulwark of the first network. Our subsequent clearances of station time have kept us at the top of agencies year after year."

(You are big and rich and right at the top, are you? So what? I don't give two whoops in Hades if you are as big as General Motors and General Electric and the General Staff of the U. S. Army all combined. If you had as much sense as a half-witted hummingbird, you would realize that I am interested in how big *I* am—not how big you are. All this talk about your enormous success makes me feel small and unimportant.)

"We desire to service our accounts with the last word on radio station information."

(*You* desire! *You* desire. You unmitigated ass. I'm not interested in what *you* desire or what Mussolini desires, or what Bing Crosby desires. Let me tell you once and for all that I am interested in what *I* desire—and you haven't said a word about that yet in this absurd letter of yours.)

"Will you, therefore, put the ———— company on your preferred list for weekly station information—

*every single detail that will be useful to an agency
in intelligently booking time."*

("Preferred list." You have your nerve! You make me
feel insignificant by your big talk about your company—
and then you ask me to put you on a "preferred" list,
and you don't even say "please" when you ask it.)

*"A prompt acknowledgment of this letter, giving
us your latest 'doings,' will be mutually helpful."*

(You fool! You mail me a cheap multigraphed letter—a
form letter scattered far and wide like the autumn leaves;
and you have the gall to ask me, when I am worried
about the mortgage and the hollyhocks and my blood
pressure, to sit down and dictate a personal note acknowl-
edging your multigraphed form letter—and you ask me
to do it "promptly." What do you mean, "promptly"?
Don't you know I am just as busy as you are—or, at
least, I like to *think* I am. And while we are on that
subject, who gave you the lordly right to order me
around? . . . You say it will be "mutually helpful." At
last, at last, you have begun to see my viewpoint. But you
are vague about how it will be to my advantage.)

> *Very truly yours,*
> John Blank
> *Manager Radio Department*

"P. S. The enclosed reprint from the Blankville
Journal *will be of interest to you and you may want
to broadcast it over your station."*

(Finally, down here in the postscript, you mention something that may help me solve one of my problems. Why
didn't you begin your letter with—but what's the use?
Any advertising man who is guilty of perpetrating such
drivel as you have sent me has something wrong with
his medulla oblongata. You don't need a letter giving our

latest doings. What you need is a quart of iodine in your
thyroid gland.)

Now if a man who devotes his life to advertising and
who poses as an expert in the art of influencing people
to buy—if he writes a letter like that, what can we expect
from the butcher and baker and carpet-tack maker?

Here is another letter, written by the superintendent
of a large freight terminal to a student of this course, Mr.
Edward Vermylen. What effect did this letter have on the
man to whom it was addressed? Read it and then I'll tell
you.

A. Zerega's Sons, Inc.,
28 Front Street,
Brooklyn, N. Y.

                    Attention: Mr. Edward Vermylen
Gentlemen:
    The operations at our outbound-rail-receiving sta-
tion are handicapped because a material percentage
of the total business is delivered us in the late afternoon. This condition results in congestion, overtime
on the part of our forces, delays to trucks, and in
some cases delays to freight. On November 10, we
received from your company a lot of 510 pieces,
which reached here at 4:20 P.M.
    We solicit your co-operation toward overcoming
the undesirable effects arising from late receipt of
freight. May we ask that, on days on which you ship
the volume which was received on the above date,
effort be made either to get the truck here earlier or
to deliver us part of the freight during the forenoon?
    The advantage that would accrue to you under
such an arrangement would be that of more expeditious discharge of your trucks and the assurance
that your business would go forward on the date of
its receipt.

                    Very truly yours,
                         J——— B———, *Supt.*

After reading this letter, Mr. Vermylen, sales manager for A. Zerega's Sons, Inc., sent it to me with the following comment:

"This letter had the reverse effect from that which was intended. The letter begins by describing the Terminal's difficulties, in which we are not interested, generally speaking. Our co-operation is then requested without any thought as to whether it would inconvenience us, and then, finally, in the last paragraph, the fact is mentioned that if we do co-operate it will mean more expeditious discharge of our trucks with the assurance that our freight will go forward on the date of its receipt.

"In other words, that in which we are most interested is mentioned last and the whole effect is one of raising a spirit of antagonism rather than of co-operation."

Let's see if we can't rewrite and improve this letter. Let's not waste any time talking about our problems. As Henry Ford admonishes, let's "get the other person's point of view and see things from his angle as well as from our own."

Here is one way of revising it. It may not be the best way; but isn't it an improvement?

Mr. Edward Vermylen,
c/o A. Zerega's Sons, Inc.,
28 Front Street,
Brooklyn, N. Y.

Dear Mr. Vermylen:
    Your company has been one of our good customers for fourteen years. Naturally, we are very grateful for your patronage and are eager to give you the speedy, efficient service you deserve. However, we regret to say that it isn't possible for us to do that when your trucks bring us a large shipment late in the afternoon, as they did on November 10. Why? Because many other customers make late afternoon deliveries also. Naturally, that causes

congestion. That means your trucks are held up un-
avoidably at the pier and sometimes even your
freight is delayed.

That's bad. Very bad. How can it be avoided?
By making your deliveries at the pier in the forenoon when possible. That will enable your trucks to
keep moving, your freight will get immediate attention, and our workmen will get home early at night
to enjoy a dinner of the delicious macaroni and
noodles that you manufacture.

Please don't take this as a complaint, and please
don't feel I am assuming to tell you how to run your
business. This letter is prompted solely by a desire
to serve you more effectively.

Regardless of when your shipments arrive, we
shall always cheerfully do all in our power to serve
you promptly.

You are busy. Please don't trouble to answer
this note.

Yours truly,
J—— B——, Supt.

Thousands of salesmen are pounding the pavements
today, tired, discouraged, and underpaid. Why? Because
they are always thinking only of what they want. They
don't realize that neither you nor I want to buy anything.
If we did, we would go out and buy it. But both of us are
eternally interested in solving our problems. And if a
salesman can show us how his services or his merchan-
dise will help us solve our problems, he won't need to
sell us. We'll buy. And a customer likes to feel that he
is buying—not being sold.

Yet many men spend a lifetime in selling without seeing
things from the customer's angle. For example, I live in
Forest Hills, a little community of private homes in the
center of greater New York. One day as I was rushing
to the station, I chanced to meet a real-estate operator
who had bought and sold property on Long Island for
many years. He knew Forest Hills well so I hurriedly
asked him whether or not my stucco house was built with

metal lath or hollow tile. He said he didn't know and told me what I already knew: that I could find out by calling the Forest Hills Gardens Association. The following morning, I received a letter from him. Did he give me the information I wanted? He could have gotten it in sixty seconds by a telephone call. But he didn't. He told me again that I could get it by telephoning myself, and then asked me to let him handle my insurance.

He was not interested in helping me. He was interested only in helping himself.

I ought to have given him copies of Vash Young's excellent little books, *The Go-Giver* and *A Fortune to Share*. If he read those books and practiced their philosophy, they would make him a thousand times as much profit as handling my insurance.

Professional men make the same mistake. Several years ago, I walked into the office of a well-known nose-and-throat specialist in Philadelphia. Before he even looked at my tonsils, he asked me what my business was. He wasn't interested in the size of my tonsils. He was interested in the size of my exchequer. His chief concern was not in how much he could help me. His chief concern was in how much he could get out of me. The result was he got nothing. I walked out of his office with contempt for his lack of character.

The world is full of people like that: grabbing, self-seeking. So the rare individual who unselfishly tries to serve others has an enormous advantage. He has little competition. Owen D. Young said: "The man who can put himself in the place of other men, who can understand the workings of their minds, need never worry about what the future has in store for him."

If out of reading this book you get just one thing: an increased tendency to think always in terms of the other person's point of view, and see things from his angle—if you get that one thing out of this book, it may easily prove to be one of the milestones of your career.

Most men go through college and learn to read Virgil and master the mysteries of calculus without ever discovering how their own minds function. For instance: I

once gave a course in "Effective Speaking" for the young
college men who were entering the employ of the Car-
rier Corporation, Newark, New Jersey, the organization
that cools office buildings and air-conditions theatres. One
of the men wanted to persuade the other to play basketball and this is about what he said: "I want you men
to come out and play basketball. I like to play basketball
but the last few times I have been to the gymnasium there
haven't been enough men there to get up a game. Two or
three of us got to throwing the ball around the other
night—and I got a black eye. I wish you boys would
come down tomorrow night. I want to play basketball."

Did he talk about anything you want? You don't want
to go to a gymnasium that no one else goes to, do you?
You don't care about what he wants. You don't want to
get a black eye.

Could he have shown you how to get the things you
want by using the gymnasium? Surely. More pep. Keener
edge to the appetite. Clearer brain. Fun. Games. Basketball.

To repeat Professor Overstreet's wise advice: "First
arouse in the other person an eager want. He who can
do this has the whole world with him. He who cannot
walks a lonely way."

One of the students in the author's training course
was worried about his little boy. The child was under-
weight and refused to eat properly. His parents used the
usual method. They scolded and nagged. "Mother wants
you to eat this and that." "Father wants you to grow up
to be a big man."

Did the boy pay any attention to these pleas? Just
about as much as you pay to one fleck of sand on a sandy
beach.

No man with a trace of horse sense would expect a
child three years old to react to the viewpoint of a
father thirty years old. Yet that was precisely what that
father had expected. It was absurd. He finally saw that.
So he said to himself: "What does that boy want? How
can I tie up what I want to what he wants?"

It was easy when he started thinking about it. His boy

had a tricycle which he loved to ride up and down the sidewalk in front of the house in Brooklyn. A few doors down the street lived a "menace," as they say out in Hollywood—a bigger boy who would pull the little boy off his tricycle and ride it himself.

Naturally, the little boy would run screaming to his mother, and she would have to come out and take the "menace" off the tricycle and put her little boy on again. This happened almost every day.

What did the little boy want? It didn't take a Sherlock Holmes to answer that one. His pride, his anger, his desire for a feeling of importance—all the strongest emotions in his make-up—goaded him on to get revenge, to smash the "menace" in the nose. And when his father told him he could wallop the daylights out of the bigger kid someday if he would only eat the things his mother wanted him to eat—when his father promised him that, there was no longer any problem of dietetics. That boy would have eaten spinach, sauerkraut, salt mackerel, anything in order to be big enough to whip the bully who had humiliated him so often.

After solving that problem, the father tackled another: the little boy had the unholy habit of wetting his bed.

He slept with his grandmother. In the morning, his grandmother would wake up and feel the sheet and say: "Look, Johnny, what you did again last night."

He would say: "No, I didn't do it. You did it."

Scolding, spankling, shaming him, reiterating that mother didn't want him to do it—none of these things kept the bed dry. So the parents asked: "How can we make this boy *want* to stop wetting his bed?"

What were his wants? First, he wanted to wear pajamas like daddy instead of wearing a nightgown like grandmother. Grandmother was getting fed up with his nocturnal iniquities so she gladly offered to buy him a pair of pajamas if he would reform. Second, he wanted a bed of his own. Grandma didn't object.

His mother took him down to Loeser's department store in Brooklyn, winked at the salesgirl, and said: "Here is a little gentleman who would like to do some shopping."

The salesgirl made him feel important by saying: "Young man, what can I show you?"

He stood a couple of inches taller and said: "I want to buy a bed for myself."

When he was shown the one his mother wanted him to buy, she winked at the salesgirl and the boy was persuaded to buy it.

The bed was delivered the next day; and that night, when father came home, the little boy ran to the door shouting: "Daddy! Daddy! Come upstairs and see *my* bed that *I* bought!"

The father, looking at the bed, obeyed Charles Schwab's injunction: he was "hearty in his approbation and lavish in his praise."

"You are not going to wet this bed, are you?" the father asked.

"Oh, no, no! I am not going to wet this bed." The boy kept his promise, for his pride was involved. That was *his* bed. *He* and *he* alone had bought it. And he was wearing pajamas now like a little man. He wanted to act like a man. And he did.

Another father, K. T. Dutschmann, a telephone engineer, a student of this course, couldn't get his three-year-old daughter to eat breakfast food. The usual scolding, pleading, coaxing methods had all ended in futility. So the parents asked themselves: "How can we make her *want* to do it?"

The little girl loved to imitate her mother, to feel big and grown up; so one morning they put her on a chair and let her make the breakfast food. At just the psychological moment, father drifted into the kitchen while she was stirring the breakfast food and she said: "Oh, look, Daddy, I am making the Maltex this morning."

She ate two helpings of the cereal that morning without any coaxing because she was interested in it. She had achieved a feeling of importance; she had found in making the breakfast food an avenue of self-expression.

William Winter once remarked that "self-expression is the dominant necessity of human nature." Why can't we use that same psychology in business? When we have a brilliant idea, instead of making the other person think it is ours, why not let him cook and stir the idea himself? He will then regard it as his own; he will like it and maybe eat a couple of helpings of it.

Remember: "First arouse in the other person an eager want. He who can do this has the whole world with him. He who cannot walks a lonely way."

Chapter 11

DO THIS AND YOU'LL BE WELCOME
ANYWHERE

Why read this book to find out how to win friends? Why not study the technique of the greatest winner of friends the world has ever known? Who is he? You may meet him tomorrow coming down the street. When you get within ten feet of him, he will begin to wag his tail. If you stop and pat him, he will almost jump out of his skin to show you how much he likes you. And you know that behind this show of affection on his part, there are no ulterior motives: he doesn't want to sell you any real estate, and he doesn't want to marry you.

Did you ever stop to think that a dog is the only animal that doesn't have to work for a living? A hen has to lay eggs; a cow has to give milk; and a canary has to sing. But a dog makes his living by giving you nothing but love.

When I was five years old, my father bought a little yellow-haired pup for fifty cents. He was the light and joy of my childhood. Every afternoon about four-thirty, he would sit in the front yard with his beautiful eyes staring steadfastly at the path, and as soon as he heard my voice or saw me swinging my dinner pail through the buck brush, he was off like a shot, racing breathlessly up the hill to greet me with leaps of joy and barks of sheer ecstasy.

Tippy was my constant companion for five years. Then one tragic night—I shall never forget it—he was killed within ten feet of my head, killed by lightning. Tippy's death was the tragedy of my boyhood.

You never read a book on psychology, Tippy. You didn't need to. You knew by some divine instinct that one can make more friends in two months by becoming genuinely interested in other people than one can in two years by trying to get other people interested in him. Let me repeat that. *You can make more friends in two months by becoming interested in other people than you can in two years by trying to get other people interested in you.*

Yet I know and you know people who blunder through life trying to wigwag other people into becoming interested in them.

Of course, it doesn't work. People are not interested in you. They are not interested in me. They are interested in themselves—morning, noon, and after dinner.

The New York Telephone Company made a detailed study of telephone conversations to find out which word is the most frequently used. You have guessed it: it is the personal pronoun "I." "I." "I." It was used 3,990 times in 500 telephone conversations. "I." "I." "I." "I." "I."

When you see a group photograph that you are in, whose picture do you look for first?

If you think people are interested in you, answer this question: If you died tonight, how many people would come to your funeral?

Why should people be interested in you unless you are first interested in them? Reach for your pencil now and write your reply here:

If we merely try to impress people and get people interested in us, we will never have many true, sincere friends. Friends, real friends, are not made that way.

Napoleon tried it, and in his last meeting with Josephine he said: "Josephine, I have been as fortunate as any man ever was on this earth; and yet, at this hour, you are the only person in the world on whom I can rely." And historians doubt whether he could rely even on her.

The late Alfred Adler, the famous Viennese psychologist, wrote a book entitled *What Life Should Mean to*

You. In that book he says: "It is the individual who is not interested in his fellow men who has the greatest difficulties in life and provides the greatest injury to others. It is from among such individuals that all human failures spring."

You may read scores of erudite tomes on psychology without coming across a statement more significant for you and for me. I dislike repetition but Adler's statement is so rich with meaning that I am going to repeat it in italics:

> *It is the individual who is not interested in his fellow men who has the greatest difficulties in life and provides the greatest injury to others. It is from among such individuals that all human failures spring.*

I once took a course in short story writing at New York University and during that course the editor of *Collier's* talked to our class. He said he could pick up any one of the dozens of stories that drifted across his desk every day, and after reading a few paragraphs he could feel whether or not the author liked people. "If the author doesn't like people," he said, "people won't like his stories."

This hard-boiled editor stopped twice in the course of his talk on fiction writing, and apologized for preaching a sermon. "I am telling you," he said, "the same things your preacher would tell you. But, remember, you have to be interested in people if you want to be a successful writer of stories."

If that is true of writing fiction, you can be sure it is trebly true of dealing with people face to face.

I spent an evening in the dressing room of Howard Thurston the last time he appeared on Broadway—Thurston, the acknowledged dean of magicians. Thurston the king of legerdemain. For forty years he traveled all over the world, time and again, creating illusions, mystifying audiences, and making people gasp with astonishment. More than sixty million people paid admission to his show, and he made almost two million dollars in profit.

I asked Mr. Thurston to tell me the secret of his success. His schooling certainly had nothing to do with it, for he ran away from home as a small boy, became a hobo, rode in box cars, slept in haystacks, begged his food from door to door, and learned to read by looking out of box cars at signs along the railway.

Did he have a superior knowledge of magic? No, he told me hundreds of books had been written about legerdemain, and scores of people knew as much about it as he did. But he had two things that the others didn't have. First, he had the ability to put his personality across the footlights. He was a master showman. He knew human nature. Everything he did, every gesture, every intonation of his voice, every lifting of an eyebrow had been carefully rehearsed in advance, and his actions were timed to split seconds. But, in addition to that, Thurston had a genuine interest in people. He told me that many magicians would look at the audience and say to themselves, "Well, there is a bunch of suckers out there, a bunch of hicks; I'll fool them all right." But Thurston's method was totally different. He told me every time he entered the stage he said to himself: "I am grateful because these people come to see me. They make it possible for me to make my living in a very agreeable way. I'm going to give them the very best I possibly can."

He declared he never stepped in front of the footlights without first saying to himself over and over: "I love my audience. I love my audience." Ridiculous? Absurd? You are privileged to think about it anything you like. I am merely passing it on to you without comment as a recipe used by one of the most famous magicians of all time.

Madame Schumann-Heink told me much the same thing. In spite of hunger and heartbreak, in spite of a life filled with so much tragedy that she once attempted to kill herself and her babies—in spite of all that, she sang her way up to the top until she became perhaps the most distinguished Wagnerian singer who ever thrilled an audience; and she, too, confessed that one of the secrets of her success is that fact that she is intensely interested in people.

That too, was one of the secrets of Theodore Roosevelt's astonishing popularity. Even his servants loved him. His colored valet, James E. Amos, wrote a book about him entitled *Theodore Roosevelt, Hero to His Valet.* In that book, Amos relates this illuminating incident:

> My wife one time asked the President about a bobwhite. She had never seen one and he described it to her fully. Some time later, the telephone at our cottage rang. [Amos and his wife lived in a little cottage on the Roosevelt estate at Oyster Bay.] My wife answered it and it was Mr. Roosevelt himself. He had called her, he said, to tell her that there was a bobwhite outside her window and that if she would look out she might see it. Little things like that were so characteristic of him. Whenever he went by our cottage, even though we were out of sight, we would hear him call out: "Oo-oo-oo, Annie!" or "Oo-oo-oo, James!" It was just a friendly greeting as he went by.

How could employees keep from liking a man like that? How could anyone keep from liking him?

Roosevelt called at the White House one day when the President and Mrs. Taft were away. His honest liking for humble people was shown by the fact that he greeted all the old White House servants by name, even the scullery maids.

"When he saw Alice, the kitchen maid," writes Archie Butt, "he asked her if she still made corn bread. Alice told him that she sometimes made it for the servants, but no one ate it upstairs.

" 'They show bad taste,' Roosevelt boomed, 'and I'll tell the President so when I see him.'

"Alice brought a piece to him on a plate, and he went over to the office eating it as he went and greeting gardeners and laborers as he passed. . . .

"He addressed each person just as he was wont to address him in the past. They still whisper about it to each other, and Ike Hoover said with tears in his eyes: 'It is the only happy day we have had in nearly two years, and not one of us would exchange it for a hundred-dollar bill.' "

It was the same intense interest in the problems of other people that made Dr. Charles W. Eliot one of the most successful presidents who ever directed a university —and you will recall that he presided over the destinies of Harvard from four years after the close of the Civil War until five years before the outbreak of World War I. Here is an example of the way Dr. Eliot worked. One day a freshman, L. R. G. Crandon, went to the president's office to borrow fifty dollars from the Students' Loan Fund. The loan was granted. "Then I made my heartfelt thanks and started to leave"—I am quoting Crandon's own words now—"when President Eliot said, 'Pray be seated.' Then he proceeded, to my amazement, to say in effect: 'I am told that you cook and eat in your room. Now I don't think that is at all bad for you if you get the right food and enough of it. When I was in college, I did the same. Did you ever make veal loaf? That, if made from sufficiently mature and sufficiently cooked veal, is one of the best things you could have, because there is no waste. This is the way I used to make it.' He then told me how to pick the veal, how to cook it slowly, with such evaporation that the soup would turn into jelly later, then how to cut it up and press it with one pan inside another and eat it cold."

I have discovered from personal experience that one can win the attention and time and co-operation of even the most sought-after people in America by becoming genuinely interested in them. Let me illustrate.

Years ago I conducted a course in fiction writing at the Brooklyn Institute of Arts and Sciences, and we wanted Kathleen Norris, Fannie Hurst, Ida Tarbell, Albert Payson Terhune, Rupert Hughes, and other distinguished and busy authors to come over to Brooklyn and give us the benefit of their experiences. So we wrote them, saying we admired their work and were deeply interested in getting their advice and learning the secrets of their success.

Each of these letters was signed by about a hundred and fifty students. We said we realized that they were busy—too busy to prepare a lecture. So we enclosed a list of questions for them to answer about themselves and their methods of work. They liked that. Who wouldn't like it? So they left their homes and traveled over to Brooklyn to give us a helping hand.

By using the same method, I persuaded Leslie M. Shaw, Secretary of the Treasury in Theodore Roosevelt's cabinet, George W. Wickersham, Attorney General in Taft's cabinet, William Jennings Bryan, Franklin D. Roosevelt, and many other prominent men to come and talk to the students of my courses in public speaking.

All of us, be we butcher or baker or the king upon his throne, all of us like people who admire us. Take the German Kaiser, for example. At the close of World War I, he was probably the most savagely and universally despised man on this earth. Even his own nation turned against him when he fled over into Holland to save his neck. The hatred against him was so intense that millions of people would have loved to have torn him limb from limb or burned him at the stake. In the midst of all this forest fire of fury, one little boy wrote the Kaiser a simple, sincere letter glowing with kindliness and admiration. This little boy said that no matter what the others thought, he would always love Wilhelm as his Emperor. The Kaiser was deeply touched by his letter and invited the little boy to come and see him. The boy came, and so did his mother—and the Kaiser married her. That little boy didn't need to read a book on "How to Win Friends and Influence People." He knew how instinctively.

If we want to make friends, let's put ourselves out to do things for other people—things that require time, energy, unselfishness, and thoughtfulness. When the Duke of Windsor was Prince of Wales, he was scheduled to tour South America, and before he started out on that tour he spent months studying Spanish so that he could make public talks in the language of the country; and the South Americans loved him for it.

For years I have made it a point to find out the birthdays of my friends. How? Although I haven't the foggiest bit of faith in astrology, I begin by asking the other party whether he believes the date of one's birth has anything to do with character and disposition. I then ask him to tell me the month and day of his birth. If he says November 24, for example, I keep repeating to myself, "November 24, November 24." The minute his back is turned, I write down his name and birthday and later transfer it to a birthday book. At the beginning of each year, I have these birthday dates scheduled in my calendar pad, so they come to my attention automatically. When the natal day arrives, there is my letter or telegram. What a hit it makes! I am frequently the only person on earth who remembers.

If we want to make friends, let's greet people with animation and enthusiasm. When somebody calls you on the telephone, use the same psychology. Say "Hello" in tones that bespeak how pleased you are to have the person call. The New York Telephone Company conducts a school to train its operators to say "Number please" in a tone that means "Good morning, I am happy to be of service to you." Let's remember that when we answer the telephone tomorrow.

Does this philosophy work in business? Does it? I could cite scores of illustrations; but we have time for only two.

Charles R. Walters, of one of the large banks in New York City, was assigned to prepare a confidential report on a certain corporation. He knew of only one man who possessed the facts he needed so urgently. Mr. Walters went to see that man, the president of a large industrial company. As Mr. Walters was ushered into the president's office, a young woman stuck her head through a door and told the president that she didn't have any stamps for him that day.

"I am collecting stamps for my twelve-year-old son," the president explained to Mr. Walters.

Mr. Walters stated his mission, and began asking questions. The president was vague, general, nebulous. He didn't want to talk, and apparently nothing could persuade him to talk. The interview was brief and barren.

"Frankly, I didn't know what to do," Mr. Walters said as he related the story to the class. "Then I remembered what his secretary had said to him—stamps, twelve-year-old son . . . And I also recalled that the foreign department of our bank collected stamps—stamps taken from letters pouring in from every continent washed by the seven seas.

"The next afternoon I called on this man and sent in word that I had some stamps for his boy. Was I ushered in with enthusiasm? Yes, sir. He couldn't have shaken my hand with more enthusiasm if he had been running for Congress. He radiated smiles and good will. 'My George will love this one,' he kept saying as he fondled the stamps. 'And look at this! This is a treasure.'

"We spent half an hour talking stamps and looking at a picture of his boy, and he then devoted more than an hour of his time to giving me every bit of information I wanted—without my even suggesting that he do it. He told me all he knew, and then called in his subordinates and questioned them. He telephoned some of his associates. He loaded me down with facts, figures, reports, and correspondence. In the parlance of newspaper men, I had a scoop."

Here is another illustration:

C. M. Knaphle, Jr., of Philadelphia, had tried for years to sell coal to a large chain-store organization. But the chain-store company continued to purchase its fuel from an out-of-town dealer and continued to haul it right past the door of Knaphle's office. Mr. Knaphle made a speech one night before one of my classes, pouring out his hot wrath upon chain stores, branding them as a curse to the nation.

And still he wondered why he couldn't sell them.

I suggested that he try different tactics. To put it briefly, this is what happened. We staged a debate between members of the course on "Resolved, that the spread of the chain store is doing the country more harm than good."

Knaphle, at my suggestion, took the negative side; he agreed to defend the chain stores, and then went straight to an executive of the chain-store organization that he despised and said: "I am not here to try to sell coal. I have come to ask you to do me a favor." He then told about his debate and said, "I have come to you for help because I can't think of anyone else who would be more capable of giving me the facts I want. I am anxious to win this debate; and I'll deeply appreciate whatever help you can give me."

Here is the rest of the story in Mr. Knaphle's own words:

I had asked this man for precisely one minute of his time. It was with that understanding that he consented to see me. After I had stated my case, he motioned me to a chair and talked to me for exactly one hour and forty-seven minutes. He called in another executive who had written a book on chain stores. He wrote to the National Chain Store Association and secured for me a copy of a debate on the subject. He feels that the chain store is rendering a real service to humanity. He is proud of what he is doing for hundreds of communities. His eyes fairly glowed as he talked; and I must confess that he opened my eyes to things I had never even dreamed of. He changed my whole mental attitude.

As I was leaving, he walked with me to the door, put his arm around my shoulder, wished me well in my debate, and asked me to stop in and see him again and let him know how I made out. The last words he said to me were: "Please see me again later in the spring. I should like to place an order with you for coal."

To me that was almost a miracle. Here he was offering to buy coal without my even suggesting it. I had made more headway in two hours by becoming genuinely interested in him and his problems than I could have made in ten years by trying to get him interested in me and my coal.

You didn't discover a new truth, Mr. Knaphle, for a long time ago, a hundred years before Christ was born, a famous old Roman poet, Publius Syrus, remarked: "We are interested in others when they are interested in us."

So if you want people to like you, the paramount rule is:

Become genuinely interested in other people.

If you want to develop a more pleasing personality, a more effective skill in human relations, let me urge you to read *The Return to Religion* by Dr. Henry Link. Don't let the title frighten you. It isn't a goody-goody book. It was written by a well-known psychologist who has personally interviewed and advised more than three thousand people who have come to him with personality problems. Dr. Link told me that he could easily have called his book *How to Develop Your Personality*. It deals with that subject. You will find it interesting, illuminating. If you read it, and act upon its suggestions, you are almost sure to increase your skill in dealing with people.

Chapter 12

HOW TO MAKE PEOPLE LIKE YOU
INSTANTLY

I was waiting in line to register a letter in the Post Office at Thirty-Third Street and Eighth Avenue in New York. I noticed that the registry clerk was bored with his job—weighing envelopes, handing out the stamps, making change, issuing receipts—the same monotonous grind year after year. So I said to myself: "I am going to try to make that chap like me. Obviously, to make him like me, I must say something nice, not about myself, but about him. So I asked myself, 'What is there about him that I can honestly admire?' " That is sometimes a hard question to answer, especially with strangers; but, in this case, it happened to be easy. I instantly saw something I admired no end.

So while he was weighing my envelope, I remarked with enthusiasm: "I certainly wish I had your head of hair."

He looked up, half-startled, his face beaming with smiles. "Well, it isn't as good as it used to be," he said modestly. I assured him that although it might have lost some of its pristine glory, nevertheless it was still magnificent. He was immensely pleased. We carried on a pleasant little conversation and the last thing he said to me was: "Many people have admired my hair."

I'll bet that chap went out to lunch that day walking on air. I'll bet he went home that night and told his wife about it. I'll bet he looked in the mirror and said: "It *is* a beautiful head of hair."

I told this story once in public; and a man asked me afterwards: "What did you want to get out of him?"

What was I trying to get out of him!!! What was I trying to get out of him!!!

If we are so contemptibly selfish that we can't radiate a little happiness and pass on a bit of honest appreciation without trying to get something out of the other person in return—if our souls are no bigger than sour crab apples, we shall meet with the failure we so richly deserve.

Oh yes, I did want something out of that chap. I wanted something priceless. And I got it. I got the feeling that I had done something for him without his being able to do anything whatever in return for me. That is a feeling that glows and sings in your memory long after the incident is passed.

There is one all-important law of human conduct. If we obey that law, we shall almost never get into trouble. In fact, that law, if obeyed, will bring us countless friends and constant happiness. But the very instant we break that law, we shall get into endless trouble. The law is this: *Always make the other person feel important.* Professor John Dewey, as we have already noted, says that the desire to be important is the deepest urge in human nature; and Professor William James says: "The deepest principle in human nature is the craving to be appreciated." As I have already pointed out, it is the urge that differentiates us from the animals. It is the urge that has been responsible for civilization itself.

Philosophers have been speculating on the rules of human relationships for thousands of years and out of all that speculation, there has evolved only one important precept. It is not new. It is as old as history. Zoroaster taught it to his fire-worshipers in Persia three thousand years ago. Confucius preached it in China twenty-four centuries ago. Lao-Tse, the founder of Taoism, taught it to his disciples in the Valley of the Han. Buddha preached it on the banks of the Holy Ganges five hundred years before Christ. The sacred books of Hinduism taught it a thousand years before that. Jesus taught it among the stony hills of Judea nineteen centuries ago. Jesus summed it up in one thought—probably the most important rule in the world: "Do unto others as you would have others do unto you."

You want the approval of those with whom you come in contact. You want recognition of your true worth. You want a feeling that you are important in your little world. You don't want to listen to cheap, insincere flattery but you do crave sincere appreciation. You want your friends and associates to be, as Charles Schwab put it, "hearty in their approbation and lavish in their praise." All of us want that.

So let's obey the Golden Rule, and give unto others what we would have others give unto us.

How? When? Where? The answer is: all the time, everywhere.

For example, I asked the information clerk in Radio City for the number of Henry Souvaine's office. Dressed in a neat uniform, he prided himself on the way he dispensed knowledge. Clearly and distinctly he replied: "Henry Souvaine. (pause) 18th floor. (pause) Room 1816."

I rushed for the elevator, then paused and went back and said: "I want to congratulate you on the splendid way you answered my question. You were very clear and precise. You did it like an artist. And that's unusual."

Beaming with pleasure, he told me why he made each pause, and precisely why each phrase was uttered as it was. My few words made him carry his necktie a bit higher; and as I shot up to the eighteenth floor, I got a feeling of having added a trifle to the sum total of human happiness that afternoon.

You don't have to wait until you are ambassador to France or chairman of the Clambake Committee of the Elks' Club before you use this philosophy of appreciation. You can work magic with it almost every day.

If, for example, the waitress brings us mashed potatoes when we ordered French fried, let's say: "I'm sorry to trouble you, but I prefer French fried." She'll reply, "No trouble at all," and will be glad to do it because you have shown respect for her.

Little phrases such as "I'm sorry to trouble you,"

"Would you be so kind as to—," "Won't you please," "Would you mind," "Thank you"—little courtesies like that oil the cogs of the monotonous grind of everyday life —and, incidentally, they are the hallmark of good breeding.

Let's take another illustration. Did you ever read any of Hall Caine's novels—*The Christian, The Deemster, The Manxman?* Millions of people read his novels, countless millions. He was the son of a blacksmith. He never had more than eight years' schooling in his life, yet when he died he was the richest literary man the world had ever known.

The story goes like this: Hall Caine loved sonnets and ballads; so he devoured all of Dante Gabriel Rossetti's poetry. He even wrote a lecture chanting the praises of Rossetti's artistic achievements—and sent a copy to Rossetti himself. Rossetti was delighted. "Any young man who has such an exalted opinion of my ability," Rossetti probably said to himself, "must be brilliant." So Rossetti invited this blacksmith's son to come to London and act as his secretary. That was the turning point in Hall Caine's life; for, in his new position, he met the literary artists of the day. Profiting by their advice and inspired by their encouragement, he launched upon a career that emblazoned his name across the sky.

His home, Greeba Castle, on the Isle of Man, became a Mecca for tourists from the far corners of the world; and he left an estate of two million, five hundred thousand dollars. Yet—who knows—he might have died poor and unknown had he not written an essay expressing his admiration for a famous man.

Such is the power, the stupendous power, of sincere, heartfelt appreciation.

Rossetti considered himself important. That is not strange. Almost everyone considers himself important, very important.

So does every nation.

Do you feel that you are superior to the Japanese? The truth is that the Japanese consider themselves far superior to you. A conservative Japanese, for example, is infuriated at the sight of a white man dancing with a Japanese lady.

Do you consider yourself superior to the Hindus in India? That is your privilege; but a million Hindus feel so infinitely superior to you that they wouldn't befoul themselves by condescending to touch food that your heathen shadow had fallen across and contaminated.

Do you feel you are superior to the Eskimos? Again, that is your privilege; but would you really like to know what the Eskimo thinks of you? Well, there are a few native hobos among the Eskimos, worthless bums who refuse to work. The Eskimos call them "white men"—that being their utmost term of contempt.

Each nation feels superior to other nations. That breeds patriotism—and wars.

The unvarnished truth is that almost every man you meet feels himself superior to you in some way; and a sure way to his heart is to let him realize in some subtle way that you recognize his importance in his little world, and recognize it sincerely.

Remember what Emerson said: "Every man I meet is in some way my superior; and in that I can learn of him."

And the pathetic part of it is that frequently those who have the least justification for a feeling of achievement bolster up their inner feeling of inadequacy by an outward shouting and tumult and conceit that are offensive and truly nauseating.

As Shakespeare put it: "Man, proud man! dressed in a little brief authority, plays such fantastic tricks before high heaven as make the angels weep."

I am going to tell you three stories of how businessmen in my own courses have applied these principles with remarkable results. Let's take the case first of a Connecticut attorney who prefers not to have his name mentioned because of his relatives.

Shortly after joining the course, Mr. R. motored down to Long Island with his wife to visit some of her relatives. She left him to chat with an old aunt of hers and then rushed off by herself to visit some of her younger relatives. Since he had to make a talk on how he had applied the principles of appreciation, he thought he would begin with the old lady. So he looked around the house to see what he could honestly admire.

"This house was built about 1890, wasn't it?" he inquired.

"Yes," she replied, "that is precisely the year it was built."

"It reminds me of the house in which I was born," he said. "It is beautiful. Well built. Roomy. You know, they don't build houses like this any more."

"You're right," the old lady agreed. "The young folks nowadays don't care for beautiful homes. All they want is a small apartment and an electric ice box and then they go off gadding about in their automobiles.

"This is a dream house," she said in a voice vibrating with tender memories. "This house was built with love. My husband and I dreamed about it for years before we built it. We didn't have an architect. We planned it all ourselves."

She then showed him about the house, and he expressed his hearty admiration for all the beautiful treasures she had picked up in her travels and cherished over a lifetime: Paisley shawls, an old English tea set, Wedgewood china, French beds and chairs, Italian paintings, and silk draperies that had once hung in a French château.

"After showing me through the house," said Mr. R., "she took me out to the garage. There, jacked up on blocks, was a Packard car—almost new."

"My husband bought that car shortly before he passed on," she said softly. "I have never ridden in it since his death. . . . You appreciate nice things, and I'm going to give this car to you."

"Why, aunty," he said, "you overwhelm me. I appreciate your generosity, of course; but I couldn't possibly accept it. I'm not even a relative of yours. I have a new car; and you have many relatives that would like to have that Packard."

"Relatives!" she exclaimed. "Yes, I have relatives who

are just waiting till I die so they can get that car. But they are not going to get it."

"If you don't want to give it to them, you can very easily sell it to a second-hand dealer," he told her.

"Sell it!" she cried. "Do you think I would sell this car? Do you think I could stand to see strangers riding up and down the street in that car—that car that my husband bought for me? I wouldn't dream of selling it. I am going to give it to you. You appreciate beautiful things!"

He tried to get out of accepting the car; but he couldn't without hurting her feelings.

This old lady, left in a big house all alone with her Paisley shawls, her French antiques, and her memories, was starving for a little recognition. She had once been young and beautiful and sought after. She had once built a house warm with love and had collected things from all over Europe to make it beautiful. Now, in the isolated loneliness of old age, she craved a little human warmth, a little genuine appreciation—and no one gave it to her. And when she found it, like a spring in the desert, her gratitude couldn't adequately express itself with anything less than the gift of a Packard car.

Let's take another case: Donald M. McMahon, superintendent of Lewis & Valentine, nurserymen and landscape architects in Rye, New York, related this incident:

"Shortly after I heard the talk on 'How to Win Friends and Influence People,' I was landscaping the estate of a famous attorney. The owner came out to give me a few suggestions about where he wished to plant a mass of rhododendrons and azaleas.

"I said, 'Judge, you have a lovely hobby. I have been admiring your beautiful dogs. I understand you win a lot of blue ribbons every year at the big dog show in Madison Square Garden.'

"The effect of this little expression of appreciation was striking.

" 'Yes,' the judge replied, 'I do have a lot of fun with my dogs. Wouldn't you like to see my kennel?'

"He spent almost an hour showing me his dogs and the prizes they had won. He even brought out their pedigrees and explained the blood lines responsible for such beauty and intelligence.

"Finally, turning to me, he asked: 'Do you have a little boy?'

" 'Yes, I do,' I replied.

" 'Well, wouldn't he like a puppy?' the judge inquired.

" 'Oh, yes, he'd be tickled pink.'

" 'All right, I am going to give him one,' the judge announced.

"He started to tell me how to feed the puppy. Then he paused. 'You'll forget it if I tell you. I'll write it out.' So the judge went in the house, typed out the pedigree and feeding instructions and gave me a puppy worth a hundred dollars and one hour and fifteen minutes of his valuable time largely because I expressed my honest admiration for his hobby and achievements."

George Eastman, of Kodak fame, invented the transparent film that made motion pictures possible, amassed a fortune of a hundred million dollars, and made himself one of the most famous businessmen on earth. Yet in spite of all these tremendous accomplishments, he craved little recognitions even as you and I.

To illustrate: A number of years ago, Eastman was building the Eastman School of Music in Rochester and also Kilbourn Hall, a theatre in memory of his mother. James Adamson, president of the Superior Seating Company of New York, wanted to get the order to supply the theatre chairs for these buildings. Phoning the architect, Mr. Adamson made an appointment to see Mr. Eastman in Rochester.

When Adamson arrived, the architect said: "I know you want to get this order; but I can tell you right now that you won't stand a ghost of a show if you take more than five minutes of George Eastman's time. He is a martinet. He is very busy. So tell your story quickly and get out."

Adamson was prepared to do just that.

When he was ushered into the room, he noticed Mr. Eastman bending over a pile of papers at his desk. Presently, Mr. Eastman looked up, removed his glasses, and walked toward the architect and Mr. Adamson, saying: "Good morning, gentlemen, what can I do for you?"

The architect introduced them and then Mr. Adamson said:

> While we have been waiting for you, Mr. Eastman, I have been admiring your office. I wouldn't mind working myself if I had a room like this to work in. You know I am in the interior-woodworking business myself, and I never saw a more beautiful office in all my life.

George Eastman replied:

> You remind me of something I had almost forgotten. It is beautiful, isn't it? I enjoyed it a great deal when it was first built. But I come down here now with a lot of other things on my mind and sometimes don't even see the room for weeks at a time.

Adamson walked over and rubbed his hand across a panel. "This is English oak, isn't it? A little different texture from Italian oak."

"Yes," Eastman replied. "That is imported English oak. It was selected for me by a friend who specializes in fine woods."

Then Eastman showed him about the room, pointing out the proportions, the coloring, the hand carving and other effects that he had helped to plan and execute.

While drifting about the room, admiring the woodwork, they paused before a window and George Eastman, in his modest, soft-spoken way, pointed out some of the institutions through which he was trying to help humanity: the University of Rochester, the General Hospital, the Homeopathic Hospital, the Friendly Home, the Children's Hospital. Mr. Adamson congratulated him warmly on the idealistic way he was using his wealth to alleviate the sufferings of humanity. Presently George Eastman unlocked a glass case and pulled out the first camera he had ever owned—an invention he had bought from an Englishman.

Adamson questioned him at length about his early struggles to get started in business, and Mr. Eastman spoke with real feeling about the poverty of his childhood, told how his widowed mother had kept a boardinghouse while he clerked in an insurance office for fifty cents a day. The terror of poverty haunted him day and night and he resolved to make enough money so his mother wouldn't have to work herself to death in a boarding-house. Mr. Adamson drew him out with further questions and listened, absorbed, while he related the story of his experiments with dry photographic plates. He told how he had worked in an office all day, and sometimes experimented all night, taking only brief naps while the chemicals were working, sometimes working and sleeping in his clothes for seventy-two hours at a stretch.

James Adamson had been ushered into Eastman's office at 10:15, and warned that he must not take more than five minutes; but an hour passed, two hours passed. They were still talking.

Finally, George Eastman turned to Adamson and said, "The last time I was in Japan I bought some chairs, brought them home, and put them in my sun porch. But the sun peeled the paint, so I went downtown the other day and bought some paint and painted the chairs myself. Would you like to see what sort of a job I can do painting chairs? All right. Come up to my home and have lunch with me and I'll show you."

After lunch, Mr. Eastman showed Adamson the chairs he had brought from Japan. They weren't worth more than $1.50 apiece, but George Eastman, who had made a hundred million dollars in business, was proud of them because he himself had painted them.

The order for the seats amounted to $90,000. Who do you suppose got the order—James Adamson or one of his competitors?

From that time on until Mr. Eastman's death, he and James Adamson were close friends.

*   *   *

Where should you and I begin applying this magic touchstone of appreciation? Why not begin right at home? I don't know of any other place where it is more needed —or more neglected. Your wife must have some good points—at least you once thought she had or you wouldn't have married her. But how long has it been since you expressed your admiration for her attractions? How long???? How long????

I was fishing up on the headwaters of the Miramichi in New Brunswick a few years ago. I was isolated in a lonely camp deep in the Canadian woods. The only thing I could find to read was a country newspaper. I read everything in it, including the ads and an article by Dorothy Dix. Her article was so fine that I cut it out and kept it. She claimed she was tired of always hearing lectures to brides. She declared that someone ought to take the bridegroom to one side and give this bit of sage advice:

Never get married until you have kissed the Blarney Stone. Praising a woman before marriage is a matter of inclination. But praising one after you marry her is a matter of necessity—and personal safety. Matrimony is no place for candor. It is a field for diplomacy.

If you wish to fare sumptuously every day, never knock your wife's housekeeping or make invidious comparisons between it and your mother's. But, on the contrary, be forever praising her domesticity and openly congratulate yourself upon having married the only woman who combines the attractions of Venus and Minerva and Mary Ann. Even when the steak is leather and the bread a cinder, don't complain. Merely remark that the meal isn't up to her usual standard of perfection, and she will make a burnt offering of herself on the kitchen stove to live up to your ideal of her.

Don't begin this too suddenly—or she'll be suspicious. But tonight, or tomorrow night, bring her some flowers or a box of candy. Don't merely say, "Yes, I ought to do it." *Do it!* And bring her a smile in addition, and some warm words of affection. If more wives and more husbands did that, I wonder if we should still have one marriage out of every six shattered on the rocks of Reno?

Would you like to know how to make a woman fall in love with you? Well, here is the secret. This is going to be good. It is not my idea. I borrowed it from Dorothy Dix. She once interviewed a celebrated bigamist who had won the hearts and savings-bank accounts of twenty-three women. (And, by the way, it ought to be noted in passing that she interviewed him in jail.) When she asked him his recipe for making women fall in love with him, he said it was no trick at all: all you had to do was to talk to a woman about herself.

And the same technique works with men: "Talk to a man about himself," said Disraeli, one of the shrewdest men who ever ruled the British Empire, "talk to a man about himself and he will listen for hours."

So if you want people to like you, use this rule:

Make the other person feel important—and do it sincerely.

You've been reading this book long enough. Close it now, knock the dead ashes out of your pipe, and begin to apply this philosophy of appreciation at once on the person nearest you—and watch the magic work.

Part Three

Ways to Win
People
to Your Way
of Thinking

Dale Carnegie said, "Most men . . . lack (the) subtle ability to enter the citadel of a man's beliefs arm-in-arm with the owner." It is in the development of this subtle ability that the secret lies if you are to learn "How to Win People to Your Way of Thinking and Get Enthusiastic Cooperation."

Chapter 13

A SURE WAY OF MAKING ENEMIES—AND HOW TO AVOID IT

When Theodore Roosevelt was in the White House, he confessed that if he could be right 75 per cent of the time, he would reach the highest measure of his expectations.

If that was the highest rating that one of the most distinguished men of the twentieth century could hope to obain, what about you and me?

If you can be sure of being right only 55 per cent of the time, you can go down to Wall Street, make a million dollars a day, buy a yacht, and marry a chorus girl. And if you can't be sure of being right even 55 per cent of the time, why should you tell other people they are wrong?

You can tell a man he is wrong by a look or an intonation or a gesture just as eloquently as you can in words—and if you tell him he is wrong, do you make him want to agree with you? Never! For you have struck a direct blow at his intelligence, his judgment, his pride, his self-respect. That will make him want to strike back. But it will never make him want to change his mind. You may then hurl at him all the logic of a Plato or an Immanuel Kant, but you will not alter his opinion, for you have hurt his feelings.

Never begin by announcing, "I am going to prove so-and-so to you." That's bad. That's tantamount to saying: "I'm smarter than you are. I'm going to tell you a thing or two and make you change your mind."

That is a challenge. That arouses opposition, and makes the listener want to battle with you before you even start.

It is difficult, under even the most benign conditions, to change people's minds. So why make it harder? Why handicap yourself?

If you are going to prove anything, don't let anybody know it. Do it so subtly, so adroitly that no one will feel that you are doing it.

> "Men must be taught as if you taught them not
> And things unknown proposed as things forgot."

As Lord Chesterfield said to his son:

> Be wiser than other people, if you can; but do not tell them so.

I believe now hardly anything that I believed twenty years ago—except the multiplication table; and I begin to doubt even that when I read about Einstein. In another twenty years, I may not believe what I have said in this book. I am not so sure now of anything as I used to be. Socrates said repeatedly to his followers in Athens: "One thing only I know; and that is that I know nothing."

Well, I can't hope to be any smarter than Socrates; so I have quit telling people they are wrong. And I find that it pays.

If a man makes a statement that you think is wrong—yes, even that you know is wrong—isn't it better to begin by saying: "Well, now, look! I thought otherwise, but I may be wrong. I frequently am. And if I am wrong, I want to be put right. Let's examine the facts"?

There's magic, positive magic, in such phrases as: "I may be wrong. I frequently am. Let's examine the facts."

Nobody in the heavens above or on the earth beneath or in the waters under the earth will ever object to your saying: "I may be wrong. Let's examine the facts."

That is what a scientist does. I once interviewed Stefansson, the famous explorer and scientist who spent eleven years up beyond the Arctic Circle and who lived on absolutely nothing but meat and water for six years. He told me of a certain experiment he had conducted and I asked him what he tried to prove by it. I shall never forget his reply. He said: "A scientist never tries to prove anything. He attempts only to find the facts."

You like to be scientific in your thinking, don't you? Well, no one is stopping you but yourself.

You will never get into trouble by admitting that you may be wrong. That will stop all argument and inspire the other fellow to be just as fair and open and broad-minded as you are. It will make him want to admit that he, too, may be wrong.

If you know positively that a man is wrong, and you tell him so bluntly, what happens? Let me illustrate by a specific case. Mr. S——, a young New York attorney, was arguing a rather important case recently before the United States Supreme Court (*Lustgarten v. Fleet Corporation* 280 U.S. 320). The case involved a considerable sum of money and an important question of law.

During the argument, one of the Supreme Court justices said to Mr. S——: "The statute of limitations in admiralty law is six years, is it not?"

Mr. S—— stopped, stared at Justice —— for a moment, and then said bluntly: "Your Honor, there is no statute of limitations in admiralty."

"A hush fell on the court," said Mr. S——, as he related his experience to one of the author's classes, "and the temperature in the room seemed to go down to zero. I was right. Justice —— was wrong. And I had told him so. But did that make him friendly? No. I still believe that I had the law on my side. And I know that I spoke better than I ever spoke before. But I didn't persuade. I made the enormous blunder of telling a very learned and famous man that he was wrong."

Few people are logical. Most of us are prejudiced and biased. Most of us are blighted with preconceived notions, with jealousy, suspicion, fear, envy, and pride. And most citizens don't want to change their minds about their religion or their haircut or Communism or Clark Gable. So, if you are inclined to tell people they are wrong, please read the following paragraph on your knees every morning before breakfast. It is from Professor James Harvey Robinson's enlightening book, *The Mind in the Making*.

> We sometimes find ourselves changing our minds without any resistance or heavy emotion, but if we are told we are wrong, we resent the imputation and harden our hearts. We are incredibly heedless in the formation of our beliefs, but find ourselves filled with an illicit passion for them when anyone proposes to rob us of their companionship. It is obviously not the ideas themselves that are dear to us, but our self-esteem which is threatened. . . . The little word "my" is the most important one in human affairs, and properly to reckon with it is the beginning of wisdom. It has the same force whether it is "my" dinner, "my" dog, and "my" house, or "my" father, "my" country, and "my" God. We not only resent the imputation that our watch is wrong, or our car shabby, but that our conception of the canals of Mars, of the pronunciation of "Epictetus," of the medicinal value of salicin, or of the date of Sargon I is subject to revision . . . We like to continue to believe what we have been accustomed to accept as true, and the resentment aroused when doubt is cast upon any of our assumptions leads us to seek every manner of excuse for clinging to it. The result is that most of our so-called reasoning consists in finding arguments for going on believing as we already do.

I once employed an interior decorator to make some draperies for my home. When the bill arrived, I caught my breath.

A few days later, a friend called and looked at the drapes. The price was mentioned and she exclaimed with a note of triumph: "What? That's awful. I am afraid he put one over on you."

True? Yes, she had told the truth, but few people like to listen to truths that reflect on their judgment. So, being human, I tried to defend myself. I pointed out that the best is eventually the cheapest, that one can't expect to get quality and artistic taste at bargain-basement prices, and so on and on.

The next day another friend dropped in, admired the draperies, bubbled over with enthusiasm, and expressed a wish that she could afford such exquisite creations for her home. My reaction was totally different. "Well, to tell the truth," I said, "I can't afford them myself. I paid too much. I'm sorry I ordered them."

When we are wrong, we may admit it to ourselves. And if we are handled gently and tactfully, we may admit it to others and even take pride in our frankness and broadmindedness. But not if someone else is trying to ram the unpalatable fact down our esophagus. . . .

Horace Greeley, the most famous editor in America during the time of the Civil War, disagreed violently with Lincoln's policies. He believed that he could drive Lincoln into agreeing with him by a campaign of argument, ridicule, and abuse. He waged this bitter campaign month after month, year after year. In fact, he wrote a brutal, bitter, sarcastic and personal attack on President Lincoln the night Booth shot him.

But did all this bitterness make Lincoln agree with Greeley? Not at all. Ridicule and abuse never do.

If you want some excellent suggestions about dealing with people and managing yourself and improving your personality, read Benjamin Franklin's autobiography—one of the most fascinating life stories ever written, one of the classics of American literature. Borrow a copy from your public library or get a copy from your bookstore. If there is no bookstore in your town, you can order one direct from Pocket Books, Inc., Mail Service Dept., 1 West 39th Street, New York, New York 10018. Ask for *The Autobiography of Benjamin Franklin,* #46334. Enclose 60¢ plus 25¢ for postage and handling.

In this autobiography, Ben Franklin tells how he conquered the iniquitous habit of argument and transformed himself into one of the most able, suave, and diplomatic men in American history.

One day, when Ben Franklin was a blundering youth, an old Quaker friend took him aside and lashed him with a few stinging truths, something like this:

Ben, you are impossible. Your opinions have a slap in them for everyone who differs with you. They have become so expensive that nobody cares for them. Your friends find they enjoy themselves better when you are not around. You know so much that no man can tell you anything. Indeed, no man is going to try, for the effort would lead only to discomfort and hard work. So you are not likely ever to know any more than you do now, which is very little.

One of the finest things I know about Ben Franklin is the way that he accepted that smarting rebuke. He was big enough and wise enough to realize it was true, to sense that he was headed for failure and social disaster. So he made a right-about-face. He began immediately to change his insolent, bigoted ways.

"I made it a rule," said Franklin, "to forbear all direct contradiction to the sentiments of others, and all positive assertion of my own. I even forbade myself the use of every word or expression in the language that imported a fix'd opinion, such as 'certainly,' 'undoubtedly,' etc., and I adopted, instead of them, 'I conceive,' 'I apprehend,' or 'I imagine' a thing to be so or so; or 'it so appears to me at present.' When another asserted something that I thought an error, I deny'd myself the pleasure of contradicting him abruptly, and of showing immediately some absurdity in his proposition: and in answering I began by observing that in certain cases or circumstances his opinion would be right, but in the present case there appear'd or seem'd to me some difference, etc. I soon found the advantage of this change in my manner; the conversations I engag'd in went on more pleasantly. The modest way in which I propos'd my opinions procur'd them a readier reception and less contradiction; I had less mortification when I was found to be in the wrong, and I more easily prevail'd with others to give up their mistakes and join with me when I happened to be in the right.

"And this mode, which I at first put on with some violence to natural inclination, became at length so easy, and so habitual to me, that perhaps for these fifty years past no one has ever heard a dogmatical expression escape me. And to this habit (after my character of integrity) I think it principally owing that I had early so much weight with my fellow citizens when I proposed new institutions, or alterations in the old, and so much influence in public councils when I became a member; for I was but a bad speaker, never eloquent, subject to much hesitation in my choice of words, hardly correct in language, and yet I generally carried my points."

How do Ben Franklin's methods work in business? Let's take two examples.

F. J. Mahoney, of 114 Liberty Street, New York, sells special equipment for the oil trade. He had booked an order for an important customer in Long Island. A blue print had been submitted and approved, and the equipment was in the process of fabrication. Then an unfortunate thing happened. The buyer discussed the matter with his friends. They warned him he was making a grave mistake. He had had something pawned off on him that was all wrong. It was too wide, too short, too this and too that. His friends worried him into a temper. Calling Mr. Mahoney on the phone, he swore he wouldn't accept the equipment that was already being manufactured.

"I checked things over very carefully and knew positively that we were right," said Mr. Mahoney as he told the story, "and I also knew that he and his friends didn't know what they were talking about, but I sensed that it would be dangerous to tell him so. I went out to Long Island to see him, and as I walked into his office, he leaped to his feet and came toward me, talking rapidly. He was so excited that he shook his fist as he talked. He condemned me and my equipment and ended up by saying, 'Now, what are you going to do about it?'

"I told him very calmly that I would do anything he said. 'You are the man who is going to pay for this,' I said, 'so you should certainly get what you want. However, somebody has to accept the responsibility. If you think you are right, give us a blue print and, although we have spent $2,000 making this job for you, we'll scrap that. We are willing to lose $2,000 in order to please you. However, I must warn you that if we build it as you insist, you must take the responsibility. But if you let us proceed as we planned, which we still believe is the right way, we will assume the responsibility.'

"He had calmed down by this time, and finally said: 'All right, go ahead, but if it is not right, God help you.'

"It was right, and he has already promised us another order for two similar jobs this season.

"When this man insulted me and shook his fist in my face and told me I didn't know my business, it took all the self-control I could summon up not to argue and try to justify myself. It took a lot of self-control, but it paid. If I had told him he was wrong and started an argument, there probably would have been a law suit, bitter feelings, a financial loss, and the loss of a valuable customer. Yes, I am convinced that it doesn't pay to tell a man he is wrong."

Let's take another example—and remember these cases I am citing are typical of the experiences of thousands of other men. R. V. Crowley is a salesman for the Gardner W. Taylor Lumber Company, of New York. Crowley admitted that he had been telling hard-boiled lumber inspectors for years that they were wrong. And he had won the arguments too. But it hadn't done any good. "For these lumber inspectors," said Mr. Crowley, "are like baseball umpires. Once they make a decision, they never change it."

Mr. Crowley saw that his firm was losing thousands of dollars through the arguments he won. So while taking my course, he resolved to change tactics and abandon arguments. With what results? Here is the story as he told it to the fellow members of his class:

"One morning the phone rang in my office. A hot and bothered person at the other end proceeded to inform me that a car of lumber we had shipped into his plant was entirely unsatisfactory. His firm had stopped unloading and requested that we make immediate arrangements to remove the stock from their yard. After about one-fourth of the car had been unloaded, their lumber inspector reported that the lumber was running 55 per cent below grade. Under the circumstances, they refused to accept it.

"I immediately started for his plant and on the way turned over in my mind the best way to handle the situation. Ordinarily, under such circumstances, I should have quoted grading rules and tried, as a result of my own experience and knowledge as a lumber inspector, to convince the other inspector that the lumber was actually up to grade, and that he was misinterpreting the rules in his inspection. However, I thought I would apply the principles learned in this training.

"When I arrived at the plant, I found the purchasing agent and the lumber inspector in a wicked humor, all set for an argument and a fight. We walked out to the car that was being unloaded and I requested that they continue to unload so that I could see how things were going. I asked the inspector to go right ahead and lay out the rejects, as he had been doing, and to put the good pieces in another pile.

"After watching him for a while it began to dawn on me that his inspection actually was much too strict and that he was misinterpreting the rules. This particular lumber was white pine, and I knew the inspector was thoroughly schooled in hard woods but not a competent, experienced inspector on white pine. White pine happened to be my own strong suit, but did I offer any objection to the way he was grading the lumber? None whatever. I kept on watching and gradually began to ask questions as to why certain pieces were not satisfactory. I didn't for one instant insinuate that the inspector was wrong. I emphasized that my only reason for asking was in order that we could give his firm exactly what they wanted in future shipments.

"By asking questions in a very friendly, co-operative spirit, and insisting continually that they were right in laying out boards not satisfactory to their purpose, I got him warmed up and the strained relations between us began to thaw and melt away. An occasional carefully put remark on my part gave birth to the idea in his mind that possibly some of these rejected pieces were actually within the grade that they had bought, and that their requirements demanded a more expensive grade. I was very careful, however, not to let him think I was making an issue of this point.

"Gradually his whole attitude changed. He finally admitted to me that he was not experienced on white pine and began to ask me questions about each piece as it came out of the car. I would explain why such a piece came within the grade specified, but kept on insisting that we did not want him to take it if it was unsuitable for their purpose. He finally got to the point where he felt guilty every time he put a piece in the rejected pile. And at last he saw that the mistake was on their part for not having specified as good a grade as they needed.

"The ultimate outcome was that he went through the entire carload again after I left, accepted the whole lot, and we received a check in full.

"In that one instance alone, a little tact and the determination to refrain from telling the other man he was wrong, saved my company one hundred and fifty dollars in actual cash, and it would be hard to place a money value on the good will that was saved."

By the way, I am not revealing anything in this chapter. Nineteen centuries ago, Jesus said: "Agree with thine adversary quickly."

In other words, don't argue with your customer or your husband or your adversary. Don't tell him he is wrong, don't get him stirred up, but use a little diplomacy.

And 2,200 years before Christ was born, old King Akhtoi of Egypt gave his son some shrewd advice—advice that is sorely needed today. Old King Akhtoi said one afternoon, between drinks, four thousand years ago: "Be diplomatic. It will help you gain your point."

So, if you want to win people to your way of thinking, the rule is:

Show respect for the other man's opinions. Never tell a man he is wrong.

Chapter 14

THE HIGH ROAD TO A MAN'S REASON

If your temper is aroused and you tell 'em a thing or two, you will have a fine time unloading your feelings. But what about the other fellow? Will he share your pleasure? Will your belligerent tones, your hostile attitude, make it easy for him to agree with you?

"If you come at me with your fists doubled," said Woodrow Wilson, "I think I can promise you that mine will double as fast as yours; but if you come to me and say, 'Let us sit down and take counsel together, and, if we differ from one another, understand why it is that we differ from one another, just what the points at issue are,' we will presently find that we are not so far apart after all, that the points on which we differ are few and the points on which we agree are many, and that if we only have the patience and the candor and the desire to get together, we will get together."

Nobody appreciated the truth of Woodrow Wilson's statement more than John D. Rockefeller, Jr. Back in 1915, Rockefeller was the most fiercely despised man in Colorado. One of the bloodiest strikes in the history of American industry had been shocking the state for two terrible years. Irate, belligerent miners were demanding higher wages from the Colorado Fuel & Iron Company; and Rockefeller controlled that company. Property had been destroyed, troops had been called out. Blood had been shed. Strikers had been shot, their bodies riddled with bullets.

At a time like that, with the air seething with hatred, Rockefeller wanted to win the strikers to his way of thinking. And he did it. How? Here's the story. After weeks

132

spent in making friends, Rockefeller addressed the representatives of the strikers. This speech, in its entirety, is a masterpiece. It produced astonishing results. It calmed the tempestuous waves of hate that threatened to engulf Rockefeller. It won him a host of admirers. It presented facts in such a friendly manner that the strikers went back to work without saying another word about the increase in wages for which they had fought so violently.

Here is the opening of that remarkable speech. Note how it fairly glows with friendliness.

Remember Rockefeller is talking to men who, a few days previously, wanted to hang him by the neck to a sour apple tree; yet he couldn't have been more gracious, more friendly if he had addressed a group of medical missionaries. His speech is radiant with such phrases as I am *proud* to be here, having *visited* in *your homes,* met many of your wives and children, we meet here not as strangers, but as *friends,* spirit of *mutual friendship,* our *common interests,* it is only by your courtesy that I am here.

"This is a red-letter day in my life," Rockefeller began. "It is the first time I have ever had the good fortune to meet the representatives of the employees of this great company, its officers and superintendents, together, and I can assure you that I am proud to be here, and that I shall remember this gathering as long as I live. Had this meeting been held two weeks ago, I should have stood here a stranger to most of you, recognizing a few faces. Having had the opportunity last week of visiting all the camps in the southern coal fields and of talking individually with practically all of the representatives, except those who were away; having visited in your homes, met many of your wives and children, we meet here not as strangers, but as friends, and it is in that spirit of mutual friendship that I am glad to have this opportunity to discuss with you our common interests.

"Since this is a meeting of the officers of the company and the representatives of the employees, it is only by your courtesy that I am here, for I am not so fortunate as to be either one or the other; and yet I feel that I

am intimately associated with you men, for, in a sense, I
represent both the stockholders and the directors."

Isn't that a superb example of the fine art of making
friends out of enemies?

Suppose Rockefeller had taken a different tack. Suppose he had argued with those miners and hurled devastating facts in their faces. Suppose he had told them
by his tones and insinuations that they were wrong. Suppose that, by all the rules of logic, he had proved that
they were wrong? What would have happened? More
anger would have been stirred up, more hatred, more
revolt.

> If a man's heart is rankling with discord and ill
> feeling toward you, you can't win him to your way
> of thinking with all the logic in Christendom. Scold-
> ing parents and domineering bosses and husbands
> and nagging wives ought to realize that people don't
> want to change their minds. They can't be forced or
> driven to agree with you or me. But they may pos-
> sibly be led to, if we are gentle and friendly, ever
> so gentle and ever so friendly.

Lincoln said that, in effect, more than a hundred years
ago. Here are his words:

> It is an old and true maxim that "a drop of honey
> catches more flies than a gallon of gall." So with
> men, if you would win a man to your cause, first
> convince him that you are his sincere friend. Therein
> is a drop of honey that catches his heart; which, say
> what you will, is the great high road to his reason.

Businessmen are learning that it pays to be friendly to
strikers. For example, when two thousand five hundred
employees in the White Motor Company's plant struck for
higher wages and a union shop, Robert F. Black, the
president, didn't wax wroth and condemn, and threaten
and talk of tyranny and Communists. He actually praised

the strikers. He published an advertisement in the Cleveland papers, complimenting them on "the peaceful way in which they laid down their tools." Finding the strike pickets idle, he bought them a couple of dozen baseball bats and gloves, and invited them to play ball on vacant lots. For those who preferred bowling, he rented a bowling alley.

This friendliness on President Black's part did what friendliness always does: it begot friendliness. So the strikers borrowed brooms, shovels, and rubbish carts, and began picking up matches, papers, cigarette stubs, and cigar butts around the factory. Imagine it! Imagine strikers tidying up the factory grounds while battling for higher wages and recognition of the union. Such an event had never been heard of before in the long, tempestuous history of American labor wars. That strike ended with a compromise settlement within a week—ended without any ill feeling or rancor.

Daniel Webster, who looked like a god and talked like Jehovah, was one of the most successful advocates who ever pleaded a cause; yet he ushered in his most powerful arguments with such friendly remarks as: "It will be for the jury to consider," "This may, perhaps, be worth thinking of, gentlemen," "Here are some facts that I trust you will not lose sight of, gentlemen," or "You, with your knowledge of human nature, will easily see the significance of these facts." No bulldozing. No high-pressure methods. No attempt to force his opinions on other men. Webster used the soft-spoken, quiet, friendly approach, and it helped to make him famous.

You may never be called upon to settle a strike or address a jury, but you may want to get your rent reduced. Will the friendly approach help you then? Let's see.

O. L. Straub, an engineer, wanted to get his rent reduced. And he knew his landlord was hard-boiled. "I wrote him," Mr. Straub said in a speech before the class, "notifying him that I was vacating my apartment as soon as my lease expired. The truth was I didn't want to move. I wanted to stay if I could get my rent reduced. But the situation seemed hopeless. Other tenants had tried—and failed. Everyone told me that the landlord was extremely difficult to deal with. But I said to myself, 'I am studying a course in how to deal with people, so I'll try it on him—and see how it works.'

"He and his secretary came to see me as soon as he got my letter. I met him at the door with a regular Charlie Schwab greeting. I fairly bubbled with good will and enthusiasm. I didn't begin talking about how high the rent was. I began talking about how much I liked his apartment house. Believe me, I was 'hearty in my approbation and lavish in my praise.' I complimented him on the way he ran the building, and told him I should like so much to stay for another year but I couldn't afford it.

"He had evidently never had such a reception from a tenant. He hardly knew what to make of it.

"Then he started to tell me his troubles. Complaining tenants. One had written him fourteen letters, some of them positively insulting. Another threatened to break his lease unless the landlord kept the man on the floor above from snoring. 'What a relief it is,' he said, 'to have a satisfied tenant like you.' And then without my even asking him to do it, he offered to reduce my rent a little. I wanted more, so I named the figure I could afford to pay, and he accepted without a word.

"As he was leaving, he turned to me and asked, 'What decorating can I have done for you?'

"If I had tried to get the rent reduced by the methods the other tenants were using, I am positive I should have met with the same failure they encountered. It was the friendly, sympathetic, appreciative approach that won."

Let's take another illustration. We'll take a woman this time—a woman from the Social Register—Mrs. Dorothy Day of Garden City on the sandy stretches of Long Island.

"I recently gave a luncheon to a small group of friends," said Mrs. Day. "It was an important occasion for me. Naturally, I was most eager to have everything go off smoothly. Emil, the *maître d'hôtel,* is usually my able assistant in these matters. But on this occasion he let me down. The luncheon was a failure. Emil was nowhere to be seen. He sent only one waiter to take care of us. This waiter hadn't the faintest conception of first-class service. He persisted in serving my guest of honor last. Once he served her one miserable little piece of celery on a large dish. The meat was tough; the potatoes greasy. It was horrible. I was furious. With considerable effort, I smiled through the ordeal, but I kept saying to myself, 'Just wait until I see Emil. I'll give him a piece of my mind all right."

"This happened on a Wednesday. The next night I heard a lecture on human relationships. As I listened, I realized how futile it would be to give Emil a dressing down. It would make him sullen and resentful. It would kill all desire to help me in the future. I tried to look at it from his standpoint. He hadn't bought the food. He hadn't cooked it. He couldn't help it because some of his waiters were dumb. Perhaps I had been too severe, too hasty in my wrath. So, instead of criticizing him, I decided to begin in a friendly way. I decided to open up on him with appreciation. This approach worked beautifully. I saw Emil the following day. He was defensively angry and spoiling for battle. I said, 'See here, Emil, I want you to know that it means a great deal to me to have you at my back when I entertain. You are the best *maître d'hôtel* in New York. Of course, I fully appreciate that you don't buy the food and cook it. You couldn't help what happened on Wednesday.'

"The clouds disappeared. Emil smiled, and said, 'Exactly, Madam. The trouble was in the kitchen. It was not my fault.'

"So I continued: 'I have planned other parties, Emil, and I need your advice. Do you think we had better give the kitchen another chance?'

"'Oh, certainly, Madam, of course. It might never happen again."

"The following week I gave another luncheon. Emil and I planned the menu. I cut his tip in half, and never mentioned past mistakes.

"When we arrived, the table was colorful with two dozen American beauty roses. Emil was in constant attendance. He could hardly have showered my party with more attention if I had been entertaining Queen Mary. The food was excellent and hot. The service was perfection. The *entrée* was served by four waiters instead of one. Emil personally served delicious mints to finish it off.

"As we were leaving, my guest of honor asked: 'Have you charmed that *maître d'hôtel?* I never saw such service, such attention.'

"She was right. I had charmed him with the friendly approach and sincere appreciation."

Years ago, when I was a barefooted boy walking through the woods to a country school out in northwest Missouri, I read a fable one day about the sun and the wind. They quarreled about which was the stronger and the wind said, "I'll prove I am. See that old man down there with a coat? I bet I can make him take his coat off quicker than you can."

So the sun went behind a cloud and the wind blew until it was almost a tornado, but the harder it blew the higher the old man wrapped his coat about him.

Finally, the wind calmed down and gave up; and then the sun came out from behind the cloud and smiled kindly on the old man. Presently, he mopped his brow and pulled off his coat. The sun then told the wind that gentleness and friendliness were always stronger than fury and force.

Even while I was a boy reading this fable, the truth of it was actually being demonstrated in the far-off town of Boston, an historic center of education and culture that I never dreamed of ever living to see. It was being demonstrated in Boston by Dr. A. H. B——, a physician, who thirty years later became one of my students. Here is the story as Dr. B—— related it in one of his talks before the class:

The Boston newspapers in those days screamed with fake medical advertising—the ads of professional abortionists and quack physicians who pretended to treat the diseases of men but who really preyed upon many innocent victims by frightening them with talk about "loss of manhood" and other terrible conditions. Their treatment consisted in keeping the victim filled with terror and in giving him no useful treatment at all. The abortionists had caused many deaths, but there were few convictions. Most of them paid small fines or got off through political influence.

The condition became so terrible that the good people of Boston rose up in holy indignation. Preachers pounded their pulpits, condemned the papers, and implored the help of Almighty God to stop this advertising. Civic organizations, businessmen, women's clubs, churches, young people's societies, damned and denounced—all in vain. A bitter fight was waged in the state legislature to make this disgraceful advertising illegal, but it was defeated by graft and political influence.

Dr. B—— was then chairman of the Good Citizenship Committee of the Greater Boston Christian Endeavor Union. His committee had tried everything. It had failed. The fight against these medical criminals seemed hopeless.

Then one night, after midnight, Dr. B—— tried something that apparently no one in Boston had ever thought of trying before. He tried kindness, sympathy, appreciation. He tried to make the publishers actually *want* to stop the advertising. He wrote the publisher of *The Boston Herald,* telling him how much he admired his paper. He had always read it; the news items were clean, not sensational; and the editorials were excellent. It was a splendid family paper. Dr. B—— declared that it was, in his opinion, the best paper in New England and one of the finest in America. "But," continued Dr. B——, "a friend of mine has a young daughter. He told me that his daughter read one of your advertisements aloud to him the other night, the advertisement of a professional abortionist, and then asked him what was meant by some of the phrases. Frankly, he was embarrassed. He didn't know what to say. Your paper goes into the best homes in Boston. If that happened in the home of my friend, isn't it probable that it is happening in many other homes also?

If you had a young daughter, would you want her to read those advertisements? And if she did read them and ask you about them, how could you explain?

"I am sorry that such a splendid paper as yours—almost perfect in every other way—has this one feature which makes some fathers dread to see their daughters pick it up. Isn't it probable that thousands of your other subscribers feel about it just as I do?"

Two days later the publisher of *The Boston Herald* wrote Dr. B——; the doctor kept the letter in his files for a third of a century and gave it to me when he was a member of my course. I have it in front of me now as I write. It is dated October 13, 1904.

A. H. B——, M.D.
Boston, Mass.
Dear Sir:

I really feel under obligation to you for your letter of the 11th inst., addressed to the editor of this paper, inasmuch as it has finally decided me on an action which I have had under contemplation ever since I have been in charge here.

Beginning Monday, I propose to have *The Boston Herald* absolutely expurgated of all objectionable advertising matter, as far as it is possible to do so. The medical cards, the whirling spray syringe, and like advertising, will be absolutely "killed," and all other medical advertising, which it is impossible to keep out at this time, will be so thoroughly edited that it will be absolutely inoffensive.

Again thanking you for your kind letter, which has been helpful in this respect, I beg to remain,

Yours sincerely,
W. E. Haskell,
Publisher.

Aesop was a Greek slave who lived at the court of Croesus and spun immortal fables six hundred years before Christ. Yet the truths he taught about human nature are just as true in Boston and Birmingham now as they were twenty-five centuries ago in Athens. The sun can make you take off your coat more quickly than the wind; and kindliness, the friendly approach, and appreciation can make people change their minds more readily than all the bluster and storming in Christendom.

Remember what Lincoln said: "A drop of honey catches more flies than a gallon of gall."

When you wish to win people to your way of thinking, don't forget to use this rule:

Begin in a friendly way.

Chapter 15

THE SECRET OF SOCRATES

In talking with people, don't begin by discussing the things on which you differ. Begin by emphasizing—and keep on emphasizing—the things on which you agree. Keep emphasizing—if possible—that you are both striving for the same end and your only difference is one of method and not of purpose.

Get the other person saying, "Yes, yes," at the outset. Keep him, if possible, from saying "No."

"A 'No' response," says Professor Overstreet in his book, *Influencing Human Behavior,* "is a most difficult handicap to overcome. When a person has said 'No,' all his pride of personality demands that he remain consistent with himself. He may later feel that the 'No' was ill-advised; nevertheless, there is his precious pride to consider! Once having said a thing, he must stick to it. Hence it is of the very greatest importance that we start a person in the affirmative direction."

The skillful speaker gets "at the outset a number of 'yes responses.' He has thereby set the psychological processes of his listeners moving in the affirmative direction. It is like the movement of a billiard ball. Propel it in one direction, and it takes some force to deflect it; far more force to send it back in the opposite direction.

"The psychological patterns here are quite clear. When a person says 'No' and really means it, he is doing far more than saying a word of two letters. His entire organism—glandular, nervous, muscular—gathers itself into a condition of rejection. There is, usually in minute but sometimes in observable degree, a physical withdrawal, or readiness for withdrawal. The whole neuro-muscular

142

system, in short, sets itself on guard against acceptance. Where, on the contrary, a person says 'Yes,' none of the withdrawing activities take place. The organism is in a forward-moving, accepting, open attitude. Hence the more 'Yeses' we can, at the very outset, induce, the more likely we are to succeed in capturing the attention for our ultimate proposal.

"It is a very simple technique—this yes response. And yet how much neglected! It often seems as if people get a sense of their own importance by antagonizing at the outset. The radical comes into a conference with his conservative brethren; and immediately he must make them furious! What, as a matter of fact, is the good of it? If he simply does it in order to get some pleasure out of it for himself, he may be pardoned. But if he expects to achieve something, he is only psychologically stupid.

"Get a student to say 'No' at the beginning, or a customer, child, husband, or wife, and it takes the wisdom and the patience of angels to transform that bristling negative into an affirmative."

The use of this "yes, yes" technique enabled James Eberson, teller for the Greenwich Savings Bank, New York City, to save a prospective customer who might otherwise have been lost.

"This man came in to open an account," said Mr. Eberson, "and I gave him our usual form to fill out. Some of the questions he answered willingly, but there were others he flatly refused to answer.

"Before I began the study of human relations, I should have told this prospective depositor that if he refused to give the bank this information, we should have to refuse to accept his account. I am ashamed that I have been guilty of doing that very thing in the past. Naturally, an ultimatum like that made me feel good. I had shown who was boss, that the bank's rules and regulations couldn't be flouted. But that sort of an attitude certainly didn't give a feeling of welcome and importance to the man who had walked in to give us his patronage.

"I resolved this morning to use a little horse sense. I resolved not to talk about what the bank wanted but about what the customer wanted. And above all else, I was determined to get him saying 'yes, yes' from the very start. So I agreed with him. I told him the information he refused to give was not absolutely necessary.

" 'However,' I said, 'suppose you have money in this bank at your death. Wouldn't you like to have the bank transfer it to your next of kin who is entitled to it according to law?'

" 'Yes, of course,' he replied.

" 'Don't you think,' I continued, 'that it would be a good idea to give us the name of your next of kin so that, in the event of your death, we could carry out your wishes without error or delay?'

"Again he said, 'Yes.'

"The young man's attitude softened and changed when he realized that we weren't asking for this information for our sake but for his sake. Before leaving the bank, this young man not only gave me complete information about himself but he opened, at my suggestion, a trust account naming his mother as the beneficiary for his account and he gladly answered all the questions concerning his mother also.

"I found that by getting him saying 'yes, yes' from the outset, he forgot the issue at stake and was happy to do all the things I suggested."

"There was a man on my territory that our company was most eager to sell," said Joseph Allison, salesman for Westinghouse. "My predecessor had called on him for ten years without selling anything. When I took over the territory, I called steadily for three years without getting an order. Finally, after thirteen years of calls and sales talk, we sold him a few motors. If these proved to be all right, I felt sure of an order for several hundred more. Such was my expectation.

"Right? I knew they would be all right. So when I called three weeks later, I was stepping high.

"But I didn't step high very long for the chief engineer greeted me with this shocking announcement: 'Allison, I can't buy the remainder of the motors from you.'

" 'Why?' I asked in amazement. 'Why?'

" 'Because your motors are too hot. I can't put my hand on them.'

"I knew it wouldn't do any good to argue. I had tried that sort of thing too long. So I thought of getting the 'yes, yes' response.

" 'Well, now look, Mr. Smith,' I said. 'I agree with you a hundred per cent; if those motors are running too hot, you ought not to buy any more of them. You must have motors that won't run any hotter than standards set by the regulations of the National Electrical Manufacturers Association. Isn't that so?'"

"He agreed it was. I had gotten my first 'yes.'

" 'The Electrical Manufacturers Association regulations say that a properly designed motor may have a temperature of 72 degrees Fahrenheit above room temperature. Is that correct?'

" 'Yes,' he agreed. 'That's quite correct. But your motors are much hotter.'

"I didn't argue with him. I merely asked: 'How hot is the mill room?'

" 'Oh,' he said, 'about 75 degrees Fahrenheit.'

" 'Well,' I replied, 'if the mill room is 75 degrees and you add 72 to that, that makes a total of 147 degrees Fahrenheit. Wouldn't you scald your hand if you held it under a spigot of hot water at a temperature of 147 degrees Fahrenheit?'

"Again he had to say yes.

" 'Well,' I suggested, 'wouldn't it be a good idea to keep your hands off those motors?'

" 'Well, I guess you're right,' he admitted. We continued to chat for a while. Then he called his secretary and lined up approximately $35,000 worth of business for the ensuing month.

"It took me years and cost me countless thousands of dollars in lost business before I finally learned that it doesn't pay to argue, that it is much more profitable and much more interesting to look at things from the other man's viewpoint and try to get him saying 'yes, yes.' "

Socrates, "the gadfly of Athens," was a brilliant old boy in spite of the fact that he went barefooted and married a girl of nineteen when he was bald-headed and forty. He did something that only a handful of men in all history have been able to do: he sharply changed the whole course of human thought; and now, twenty-three centuries after his death, he is honored as one of the wisest persuaders who ever influenced this wrangling world.

His method? Did he tell people they were wrong? Oh, no, not Socrates. He was far too adroit for that. His whole technique, now called the "Socratic method," was based upon getting a "yes, yes" response. He asked questions with which his opponent would have to agree. He kept on winning one admission after another until he had an armful of yeses. He kept on asking questions until finally, almost without realizing it, his opponent found himself embracing a conclusion that he would have bitterly denied a few minutes previously.

The next time we are smarting to tell a man he is wrong, let's remember barefooted old Socrates and ask a gentle question—a question that will get the "yes, yes" response.

The Chinese have a proverb pregnant with the age-old wisdom of the changeless East: "He who treads softly goes far."

They have spent five thousand years studying human nature, those cultured Chinese, and they have garnered a lot of perspicacity: "He who treads softly goes far."

If you want to win people to your way of thinking, the rule is:

Get the other person saying "yes, yes" immediately.

Chapter 16

HOW TO GET CO-OPERATION

Don't you have much more faith in ideas that you discover for yourself than in ideas that are handed to you on a silver platter? If so, isn't it bad judgment to try to ram your opinions down the throats of other people? Wouldn't it be wiser to make suggestions—and let the other man think out the conclusion for himself?

To illustrate: Mr. Adolph Seltz of Philadelphia, a student of one of my courses, suddenly found himself confronted with the necessity of injecting enthusiasm into a discouraged and disorganized group of automobile salesmen. Calling a sales meeting, he urged his men to tell him exactly what they expected from him. As they talked, he wrote their ideas on the blackboard. He then said: "I'll give you all these qualities you expect from me. Now I want you to tell me what I have a right to expect from you." The replies came quick and fast: loyalty, honesty, initiative, optimism, team work, eight hours a day of enthusiastic work. One man volunteered to work fourteen hours a day. The meeting ended with a new courage, a new inspiration, and Mr. Seltz reported to me that the increase of sales had been phenomenal.

"The men had made a sort of moral bargain with me," said Mr. Seltz, "and as long as I lived up to my part in it, they were determined to live up to theirs. Consulting them about their wishes and desires was just the shot in the arm they needed."

No man likes to feel that he is being sold something or told to do a thing. We much prefer to feel that we are buying of our own accord or acting on our own ideas.

We like to be consulted about our wishes, our wants, our thoughts.

For example, take the case of Eugene Wesson. He lost countless thousands of dollars in commissions before he learned this truth. Mr. Wesson sells sketches for a studio that creates designs for stylists and textile manufacturers. Mr. Wesson had called once a week, every week for three years, on one of the leading stylists in New York. "He never refused to see me," said Mr. Wesson, "but he never bought. He always looked over my sketches very carefully and then said: 'No, Wesson, I guess we don't get together today.'"

After a hundred and fifty failures, Wesson realized he must be in a mental rut; so he resolved to devote one evening a week to the study of influencing human behavior, and to develop new ideas and generate new enthusiasms.

Presently he was stimulated to try a new approach. Picking up half a dozen unfinished sketches the artists were working on, he rushed over to his buyer's office. "I want you to do me a little favor, if you will," he said. "Here are some uncompleted sketches. Won't you please tell me how we could finish them up in such a way that they would be of service to you?"

The buyer looked at the sketches for a while without uttering a word and then said: "Leave these with me for a few days, Wesson, and then come back and see me."

Wesson returned three days later, got his suggestions, took the sketches back to the studio and had them finished according to the buyer's ideas. The result? All accepted.

That was nine months ago. Since that time, this buyer has ordered scores of other sketches, all drawn according to his ideas—and the net result has been more than sixteen hundred dollars in commissions for Wesson. "I now realize why I failed for years to sell this buyer," said Mr. Wesson. "I had urged him to buy what I thought he ought to have. I do the very opposite now. I urge him to give me his ideas. He feels now that he is creating the designs. And he is. I don't have to sell him now. He buys."

When Theodore Roosevelt was Governor of New York, he accomplished an extraordinary feat. He kept on good terms with the political bosses and yet he forced through reforms which they bitterly disliked.

And here is how he did it.

When an important office was to be filled, he invited the political bosses to make recommendations. "At first," said Roosevelt, "they might propose a broken-down party hack, the sort of man who has to be 'taken care of.' I would tell them that to appoint such a man would not be good politics, as the public would not approve it.

"Then they would bring me the name of another party hack, a persistent office holder, who, if he had nothing against him, had little in his favor. I would tell them that this man would not measure up to the expectations of the public, and I would ask them to see if they could not find someone more obviously fitted for the post.

"Their third suggestion would be a man who was almost good enough, but not quite.

"Then I would thank them, asking them to try once more, and their fourth suggestion would be acceptable; they would then name just the sort of man I should have picked out myself. Expressing my gratitude for their assistance, I would appoint this man—*and I would let them take the credit for the appointment*. . . . I would tell them that I had done these things to please them and now it was their turn to please me."

And they did. They did it by supporting such sweeping reforms as the Civil Service Bill and the Franchise Tax Bill.

Remember, Roosevelt went to great lengths to consult the other men and show respect for their advice. When Roosevelt made an important appointment, he let the bosses really feel that they had selected the candidate, that the idea was theirs.

An automobile dealer on Long Island used this same technique to sell a used car to a Scotsman and his wife. This dealer had shown the Scotsman car after car, but there was always something wrong. This didn't suit. That was out of kilter. The price was too high. Always the price was too high. At this juncture, the dealer, a member of one of my courses, appealed to the class for help.

We advised him to quit trying to sell "Sandy" and let "Sandy" buy. We said, instead of telling "Sandy" what to do, why not let him tell you what to do? Let him feel that the idea is his.

That sounded good. So the dealer tried it a few days later when a customer wanted to trade an old car in on a new one. The dealer knew this used car might appeal to "Sandy." So, he picked up the phone and asked "Sandy" if he wouldn't, as a special favor, come over and give him a bit of advice.

When "Sandy" arrived, the dealer said: "You are a shrewd buyer. You know car values. Won't you please look over this car and try it out and tell me how much I ought to allow for it in a trade?"

"Sandy" was "one vast substantial smile." At last his advice was being sought, his ability was being recognized. He drove the car up Queens Boulevard from Jamaica to Forest Hills and back again. "If you can get that car for three hundred," he advised, "you'll be getting a bargain."

"If I can get it at that figure, would you be willing to buy it?" the dealer inquired. Three hundred? Of course. That was his idea, his appraisal. The deal was closed immediately.

This same psychology was used by an X-ray manufacturer to sell his equipment to one of the largest hospitals in Brooklyn. This hospital was building an addition, and preparing to equip it with the finest X-ray department in America. Dr. L——, who was in charge of the X-ray department, was overwhelmed with salesmen, each caroling the praises of his own equipment.

One manufacturer, however, was more skillful. He knew far more about handling human nature than the others did. He wrote a letter something like this:

Our factory has recently completed a new line of X-ray equipment. The first shipment of these machines has just arrived at our office. They are not perfect. We know that, and we want to improve them. So we should be deeply obligated to you if you could find time to look them over and give us your ideas about how they can be made more serviceable to your profession. Knowing how occupied you are, I shall be glad to send my car for you at any hour you specify.

"I was surprised to get that letter," Dr. L—— said, as he related the incident before the class. "I was both surprised and complimented. I had never had an X-ray manufacturer seeking my advice before. It made me feel important. I was busy every night that week, but I canceled a dinner appointment in order to look over that equipment. The more I studied it, the more I discovered for myself how much I liked it.

"Nobody had tried to sell it to me. I felt that the idea of buying that equipment for the hospital was my own. I sold myself on its superior qualities and ordered it installed."

Colonel Edward M. House wielded an enormous influence in national and international affairs while Woodrow Wilson occupied the White House. Wilson leaned upon Colonel House for secret counsel and advice more than he did upon even members of his own cabinet.

What method did the Colonel use in influencing the President? Fortunately, we know, for House himself revealed it to Arthur D. Howden Smith, and Smith quoted House in an article in *The Saturday Evening Post*.

"'After I got to know the President,' House said, 'I learned the best way to convert him to an idea was to plant it in his mind casually, but so as to interest him in it—so as to get him thinking about it on his own account. The first time this worked it was an accident. I had been visiting him at the White House, and urged a policy on him which he appeared to disapprove. But several days later, at the dinner table, I was amazed to hear him trot out my suggestion as his own.' "

Did House interrupt him and say, "That's not your idea. That's mine"? Oh, no. Not House. He was too adroit for that. He didn't care about credit. He wanted results. So he let Wilson continue to feel that the idea was his. House did even more than that. He gave Wilson public credit for these ideas.

Let's remember that the people with whom we come in contact tomorrow will be just as human as Woodrow Wilson. So let's use the technique of Colonel House.

A man up in New Brunswick used this technique on me a few years ago—and got my patronage. I was planning at the time to do some fishing and canoeing in New Brunswick. So I wrote the tourist bureau for information. My name and address were evidently put on a public list, for I was immediately overwhelmed with scores of letters and booklets and printed testimonials from camps and guides. I was bewildered. I didn't know which to choose. Then one camp owner did a very clever thing. He sent me the names and telephone numbers of several New York people he had served and invited me to telephone them and discover for myself what he had to offer.

I found to my surprise that I knew one of the men on his list. I telephoned him, found out what his experiences had been, and then wired the camp the date of my arrival.

The others had been trying to sell me on their service, but one chap let me sell myself. He won.

So if you want to influence people to your way of thinking:

Let the other fellow feel that the idea is his.

Twenty-five centuries ago, Lao Tse, a Chinese sage, said some things that readers of this book might use today:

"The reason why rivers and seas receive the homage of a hundred mountain streams is that they keep below them. Thus they are able to reign over all the mountain streams. So the sage, wishing to be above men, putteth himself below them; wishing to be before them, he putteth himself behind them. Thus, though his place be above men, they do not feel his weight; though his place be before them, they do not count it an injury."

Chapter 17

AN APPEAL THAT EVERYBODY LIKES

I was reared on the edge of the Jesse James country out in Missouri and I have visited the James farm at Kearney, Missouri, where the son of Jesse James is still living.

His wife told me stories of how Jesse robbed trains and held up banks and then gave money to the neighboring farmers to pay off their mortgages.

Jesse James probably regarded himself as an idealist at heart, just as Dutch Schultz, "Two Gun" Crowley, and Al Capone did two generations later. The fact is that every man you meet—even the man you see in the mirror—has a high regard for himself, and likes to be fine and unselfish in his own estimation.

J. Pierpont Morgan observed, in one of his analytical interludes, that a man usually has two reasons for doing a thing: one that sounds good and a real one.

The man himself will think of the real reason. You don't need to emphasize that. But all of us, being idealists at heart, like to think of the motives that sound good. So, in order to change people, appeal to the nobler motives.

Is that too idealistic to work in business? Let's see. Let's take the case of Hamilton J. Farrell of the Farrell-Mitchell Company of Glenolden, Pennsylvania. Mr. Farrell had a disgruntled tenant who threatened to move. The tenant's lease still had four months to run, at fifty-five dollars a month; nevertheless, he served notice that he was vacating immediately, regardless of lease.

"These people had lived in my house all winter—the most expensive part of the year," Mr. Farrell said as he told the story to the class, "and I knew it would be difficult to rent the apartment again before fall. I could see two hundred and twenty dollars going over the hill—and believe me, I saw red.

"Now, ordinarily, I would have waded into that tenant and advised him to read his lease again. I would have pointed out that if he moved, the full balance of his rent would fall due at once—and that I could, *and would,* move to collect.

"However, instead of flying off the handle and making a scene, I decided to try other tactics. So I started like this: 'Mr. Doe,' I said, 'I have listened to your story, and I still don't believe you intend to move. Years in the renting business have taught me something about human nature, and I sized you up in the first place as being a man of your word. In fact, I'm so sure of it that I'm willing to take the gamble.

"'Now, here's my proposition. Lay your decision on the table for a few days and think it over. If you come back to me between now and the first of the month, when your rent is due, and tell me you still intend to move, I give you my word I will accept your decision as final. I will privilege you to move, and admit to myself I've been wrong in my judgment. But, I still believe you're a man of your word and will live up to your contract. For after all, we are either men or monkeys and the choice usually lies with ourselves!'

"Well, when the new month came around, this gentleman came and paid his rent in person. He and his wife had talked it over, he said—and decided to stay. They had concluded that the only honorable thing to do was to live up to their lease."

When the late Lord Northcliffe found a newspaper using a picture of himself which he didn't want published, he wrote the editor a letter. But did he say, "Please do not publish that picture of me any more; *I* don't like it"? No, he appealed to a nobler motive. He appealed to the respect and love that all of us have for motherhood. He wrote, "Please do not publish that picture of me any more. *My mother* doesn't like it."

When John D. Rockefeller, Jr., wished to stop newspaper photographers from snapping pictures of his children, he, too, appealed to the nobler motives. He didn't say: "*I* don't want their pictures published." No, he appealed to the desire, deep in all of us, to refrain from harming children. He said: "You know how it is, boys. You've got children yourselves, some of you. And you know it's not good for youngsters to get too much publicity."

When Cyrus H. K. Curtis, the poor boy from Maine, was starting on his meteoric career which was destined to make him millions as owner of *The Saturday Evening Post* and the *Ladies' Home Journal*—when he first started, he couldn't afford to pay the prices that other magazines paid. He couldn't afford to hire first-class authors to write for money alone. So he appealed to their nobler motives. For example, he persuaded even Louisa May Alcott, the immortal author of *Little Women,* to write for him when she was at the flood tide of her fame; and he did it by offering to send a check for a hundred dollars, not to her, but to her favorite charity.

Right here the skeptic may say: "Oh, that stuff is all right for Northcliffe and Rockefeller or a sentimental novelist. But, boy! I'd like to see you make it work with the tough babies I have to collect bills from!"

You may be right. Nothing will work in all cases—and nothing will work with all men. If you are satisfied with the results you are now getting, why change? If you are not satisfied, why not experiment?

At any rate, I think you will enjoy reading this true story told by James L. Thomas, a former student of mine:

Six customers of a certain automobile company refused to pay their bills for servicing. No customer protested the entire bill but each one claimed that some one charge was wrong. In each case, the customer had signed for the work done, so the company knew it was right—and *said* so. That was the first mistake.

Here are the steps the men in the credit department took to collect these overdue bills. Do you suppose they succeeded?

1. They called on each customer and told him bluntly that they had come to collect a bill that was long past due.
2. They made it very plain that the company was absolutely and unconditionally right; therefore he, the customer, was absolutely and unconditionally wrong.
3. They intimated that they, the company, knew more about automobiles than he could ever hope to know. So what was the argument about?
4. Result: they argued.

Did any of these methods reconcile the customer and settle the account? You can answer that one yourself.

At this stage of affairs, the credit manager was about to open fire with a battery of legal talent, when fortunately the matter came to the attention of the general manager. The manager investigated these defaulting clients, and discovered that they all had the reputation of paying their bills promptly. Something was wrong here—something was drastically wrong about the method of collection. So he called in James L. Thomas and told him to collect these "uncollectible accounts."

These are the steps Mr. Thomas took.

1. "My visit to each customer," says Mr. Thomas, "was likewise to collect a bill long past due—a bill that we knew was absolutely right. But I didn't say a word about that. I explained I had called to find out what it was the company had done, or failed to do.
2. "I made it clear that, until I had heard the customer's story, I had no opinion to offer. I told him the company made no claims to being infallible.
3. "I told him I was interested only in his car, and that he knew more about his car than anyone else in the world; that he was the authority on the subject.

4. "I let him talk, and I listened to him with all the interest and sympathy that he wanted—and had expected.

5. "Finally, when the customer was in a reasonable mood, I put the whole thing up to his sense of fair play. I appealed to the nobler motives. 'First,' I said, 'I want you to know that I also feel this matter has been badly mishandled. You have been inconvenienced and annoyed and irritated by one of our representatives. That should never have happened. I'm sorry and, as a representative of the company, I apologize. As I sat here and listened to your side of the story, I could not help being impressed by your fairness and patience. And now, because you are fair-minded and patient, I am going to ask you to do something for me. It's something that you can do better than anyone else, something you know more about than anyone else. Here is this bill of yours; I know that it is safe for me to ask you to adjust it, just as you would do if you were the president of my company. I am going to leave it all up to you. Whatever you say goes.'

"Did he adjust the bill? He certainly did, and got quite a kick out of it. The bills ranged from $150 to $400—but did the customer give himself the best of it? Yes, one of them did! One of them refused to pay a penny of the disputed charge; but the other five all gave the company the best of it! And here's the cream of the whole thing—we delivered new cars to all six of these customers within the next two years!

"Experience has taught me," says Mr. Thomas, "that when no information can be secured about the customer, the only sound basis on which to proceed is to assume that he is sincere, honest, truthful, and willing and anxious to pay the charges, once he is convinced they are correct. To put it differently and perhaps more clearly, people are honest and want to discharge their obligations. The exceptions to that rule are comparatively few, and I am convinced that the individual who is inclined to chisel will in most cases react favorably if you make him feel that you consider him honest, upright, and fair."

So, if you want to win people to your way of thinking, it is a fine thing, in general, to follow this rule:

Appeal to the nobler motives.

Part Four

Ways to Change People Without Giving Offense or Arousing Resentment

If we intend to "Change People Without Giving Offense or Arousing Resentment," we must begin with an attitude of respect for, and acceptance of, the *person*. His response depends upon our attitude.

Chapter 18

HOW TO CRITICIZE—AND NOT BE
HATED FOR IT

Charles Schwab was passing through one of his steel mills one day at noon when he came across some of his employees smoking. Immediately above their heads was a sign which said "No smoking." Did Schwab point to the sign and say, "Can't you read?" Oh, no, not Schwab. He walked over to the men, handed each one a cigar, and said, "I'll appreciate it, boys, if you will smoke these on the outside." They knew that he knew that they had broken a rule—and they admired him because he said nothing about it and gave them a little present and made them feel important. Couldn't keep from loving a man like that, could you?

John Wanamaker used the same technique. Wanamaker used to make a tour of his great store in Philadelphia every day. Once he saw a customer waiting at a counter. No one was paying the slightest attention to her. The sales people? Oh, they were in a huddle at the far end of the counter laughing and talking among themselves. Wanamaker didn't say a word. Quietly slipping behind the counter, he waited on the woman himself and then handed the purchase to the sales people to be wrapped as he went on his way.

On March 8, 1887, the eloquent Henry Ward Beecher died, or changed worlds, as the Japanese say. The following Sunday, Lyman Abbott was invited to speak in the pulpit left silent by Beecher's passing. Eager to do his best, he wrote, rewrote, and polished his sermon with the meticulous care of a Flaubert. Then he read it to his wife. It was poor—as most written speeches are. She might have said, if she had had less judgment, "Lyman, that is terrible. That'll never do. You'll put people to sleep. It reads like an encyclopedia. You ought to know better than that after all the years you have been preaching. For heaven's sake, why don't you talk like a human being? Why don't you act natural? You'll disgrace yourself if you ever read that stuff."

That's what she *might* have said. And, if she had, you know what would have happened. And she knew too. So, she merely remarked that it would make an excellent article for the *North American Review*. In other words, she praised it and at the same time subtly suggested that it wouldn't do as a speech. Lyman Abbott saw the point, tore up his carefully prepared manuscript, and preached without even using notes.

To change people without giving offense or arousing resentment, the rule is:

Call attention to people's mistakes indirectly.

Chapter 19

TALK ABOUT YOUR OWN MISTAKES FIRST

A few years ago, my niece, Josephine Carnegie, left her home in Kansas City and came to New York to act as my secretary. She was nineteen, had graduated from high school three years previously, and her business experience was a trifle more than zero. Today she is one of the most perfect secretaries west of Suez; but, in the beginning, she was—well, susceptible to improvement. One day when I started to criticize her, I said to myself: "Just a minute, Dale Carnegie; just a minute. You are twice as old as Josephine. You have had ten thousand times as much business experience. How can you possibly expect her to have your viewpoint, your judgment, your initiative—mediocre though they may be? And just a minute, Dale, what were you doing at nineteen? Remember the asinine mistakes and blunders you made? Remember the time you did this . . . and that . . . ?"

After thinking the matter over, honestly and impartially, I concluded that Josephine's batting average at nineteen was better than mine had been—and that, I'm sorry to confess, isn't paying Josephine much of a compliment.

So after that, when I wanted to call Josephine's attention to a mistake, I used to begin by saying, "You have made a mistake, Josephine, but the Lord knows, it's no worse than many I have made. You were not born with judgment. That comes only with experience; and you are better than I was at your age. I have been guilty of so many stupid, silly things myself I have very little inclination to criticize you or anyone. But don't you think it would have been wiser if you had done so and so?"

It isn't nearly so difficult to listen to a recital of your own faults if the criticizer begins by humbly admitting that he, too, is far from impeccable.

The polished Prince von Bülow learned the sharp necessity of doing this back in 1909. Von Bülow was then the Imperial Chancellor of Germany, and on the throne sat Wilhelm II—Wilhelm, the haughty; Wilhelm, the arrogant; Wilhelm, the last of the German Kaisers, building an army and navy which he boasted could whip their weight in wild cats.

Then an astonishing thing happened. The Kaiser said things, incredible things, things that rocked the continent and started a series of explosions heard around the world. To make matters infinitely worse, the Kaiser made these silly, egotistical, absurd announcements in public, he made them while he was a guest in England, and he gave his royal permission to have them printed in the *Daily Telegraph*. For example, he declared that he was the only German who felt friendly towards the English; that he was constructing a navy against the menace of Japan; that he, and he alone, had saved England from being humbled in the dust by Russia and France; that it was *his* plan of campaign that enabled England's Lord Roberts to defeat the Boers in South Africa; and so on and on.

No other such amazing words had ever fallen from the lips of a European king in peacetime within a hundred years. The entire continent buzzed with the fury of a hornets' nest. England was incensed. German statesmen were aghast. And in the midst of all this consternation, the Kaiser became panicky, and suggested to Prince von Bülow, the Imperial Chancellor, that he take the blame. Yes, he wanted von Bülow to announce that it was all his responsibility, that he had advised his monarch to say these incredible things.

"But Your Majesty," von Bülow protested, "it seems to me utterly impossible that anybody either in Germany or England could suppose me capable of having advised Your Majesty to say any such thing."

The moment those words were out of von Bülow's

mouth, he realized he had made a grave mistake. The Kaiser blew up.

"You consider me a donkey," he shouted, "capable of blunders you yourself could never have committed!"

Von Bülow knew that he ought to have praised before he condemned; but since that was too late, he did the next best thing. He praised after he had criticized. And it worked a miracle.

"I'm far from suggesting that," he answered respectfully. "Your Majesty surpasses me in many respects; not only, of course, in naval and military knowledge, but, above all, in natural science. I have often listened in admiration when Your Majesty explained the barometer, or wireless telegraphy, or the Röntgen rays. I am shamefully ignorant of all branches of natural science, have no notion of chemistry or physics, and am quite incapable of explaining the simplest of natural phenomena. But," von Bülow continued, "in compensation, I possess some historical knowledge and perhaps certain qualities useful in politics, especially in diplomacy."

The Kaiser beamed. Von Bülow had praised him. Von Bülow had exalted him and humbled himself. The Kaiser could forgive anything after that. "Haven't I always told you," he exclaimed with enthusiasm, "that we complete one another famously? We should stick together, and we will!"

He shook hands with von Bülow, not once, but several times. And later in the day he waxed so enthusiastic that he exclaimed with doubled fists, "If anyone says anything to me against Prince von Bülow, *I shall punch him in the nose!*"

Von Bülow saved himself in time—but, canny diplomat that he was, he nevertheless had made one error: he should have *begun* by talking about his own shortcomings and Wilhelm's superiority—not by intimating that the Kaiser was a half-wit in need of a guardian.

If a few sentences humbling oneself and praising the other party can turn a haughty, insulted Kaiser into a staunch friend, imagine what humility and praise can do for you and me in our daily contacts. Rightfully used, they will work veritable miracles in human relations.

To change people without giving offense or arousing resentment, the rule is:

Talk about your own mistakes before criticizing the other person.

Chapter 20

NO ONE LIKES TO TAKE ORDERS

I once had the pleasure of dining with Miss Ida Tarbell, the dean of American biographers. When I told her I was writing this book, we began discussing this all-important subject of getting along with people, and she told me that while she was writing her biography of Owen D. Young she interviewed a man who had sat for three years in the same office with Mr. Young. This man declared that during all that time he had never heard Owen D. Young give a direct order to anyone. He always gave suggestions, not orders. Owen D. Young never said, for example, "Do this or do that," or "Don't do this or don't do that." He would say, "You might consider this," or "Do you think that would work?" Frequently he would say, after he had dictated a letter, "What do you think of this?" In looking over a letter of one of his assistants, he would say, "Maybe if we were to phrase it this way it would be better." He always gave a person an opportunity to do things himself; he never told his assistants to do things; he let them do them, let them learn from their mistakes.

A technique like that makes it easy for a person to correct his error. A technique like that saves a man's pride and gives him a feeling of importance. It makes him want to co-operate instead of rebel.

To change people without giving offense or arousing resentment, another rule is:

Ask questions instead of giving direct orders.

169

Chapter 21

LET THE OTHER MAN SAVE HIS FACE

Years ago the General Electric Company was faced with the delicate task of removing Charles Steinmetz from the head of a department. Steinmetz, a genius of the first magnitude when it came to electricity, was a washout as the head of the calculating department. Yet the company didn't dare offend the man. He was indispensable—and highly sensitive. So they gave him a new title. They made him Consulting Engineer of the General Electric Company—a new title for work he was already doing—and let someone else head up the department.

Steinmetz was happy.

So were the officers of the G. E. They had gently maneuvered their most temperamental star, and they had done it without a storm—by letting him save his face.

Letting him save his face! How important, how vitally important that is! And how few of us ever stop to think of it! We ride roughshod over the feelings of others, getting our own way, finding fault, issuing threats, criticizing a child or an employee in front of others, without even considering the hurt to the other person's pride! Whereas a few minutes' thought, a considerate word or two, a genuine understanding of the other person's attitude would go so far towards alleviating the sting!

Let's remember that the next time we are faced with the distasteful necessity of discharging a servant or an employee.

"Firing employees is not much fun. Getting fired is even less fun." (I'm quoting now from a letter written me by Marshall A. Granger, certified public accountant.)

"Our business is mostly seasonal. Therefore we have to let a lot of men go in March.

"It's a byword in our profession that no one enjoys wielding the ax. Consequently, the custom has developed of getting it over as soon as possible, and usually in the following way: 'Sit down, Mr. Smith. The season's over, and we don't seem to see any more assignments for you. Of course, you understood that you were only employed for the busy season anyhow, etc. etc.'

"The effect on the men was one of disappointment, and a feeling of being 'let down.' Most of them were in the accounting field for life, and they retained no particular love for the firm that dropped them so casually.

"I recently decided to let our extra men go with a little more tact and consideration. So I have called each man in only after carefully thinking over his work during the winter. And I've said something like this: 'Mr. Smith, you've done a fine job (if he has). That time we sent you over to Newark, you had a tough assignment. You were on the spot, but you came through with flying colors, and we want you to know the firm is proud of you. You've got the stuff—you're going a long way, wherever you're working. This firm believes in you, and is rooting for you, and we don't want you to forget it!'

"Effect? The men go away feeling a lot better about being fired. They don't feel 'let down.' They know if we had work for them, we'd keep them on. And when we need them again, they come to us with a keen personal affection."

The late Dwight Morrow possessed an uncanny ability to reconcile belligerents who wanted to fly at each other's throats. How? He scrupulously sought what was right and just on both sides—he praised it, emphasized it, brought it carefully to the light—and no matter what the settlement, he never placed any man in the wrong.

That's what every arbitrator knows—let men save their faces.

Really big men, the world over, are too big to waste time gloating over their personal triumphs. To illustrate:

In 1922, after centuries of bitter antagonism, the Turks determined to drive the Greeks forever from Turkish territory.

Mustapha Kemal made a Napoleonic speech to his soldiers, saying, "Your goal is the Mediterranean," and one of the bitterest wars in modern history was on. The Turks won; and when the two Greek generals, Tricoupis and Dionis, made their way to Kemal's headquarters to surrender, the Turkish people called down the curses of heaven upon their vanquished foes.

But Kemal's attitude was free from triumph.

"Sit down, gentlemen," he said, grasping their hands. "You must be tired." Then, after discussing the campaign in detail, he softened the blow of their defeat. "War," he said, as one soldier to another, "is a game in which the best men are sometimes worsted."

Even in the full flush of victory, Kemal remembered this important rule:

Let the other man save his face.

IN A NUTSHELL

RULES FROM HOW TO STOP WORRYING AND START LIVING

1. Do not imitate others.
2. Apply these four good working habits:
   a. Clear your desk of all papers except those relating to the immediate problem at hand.
   b. Do things in the order of their importance.
   c. When you face a problem, solve it then and there if you have the facts necessary to make a decision.
   d. Learn to organize, deputize, and supervise.
3. Learn to relax at your work.
4. Put enthusiasm into your work.
5. Count your blessings—not your troubles.
6. Remember that unjust criticism is often a disguised compliment.
7. Do the very best you can.

RULES FROM HOW TO WIN FRIENDS AND INFLUENCE PEOPLE

1. Don't criticize, condemn or complain.
2. Give honest, sincere appreciation.
3. Arouse in the other person an eager want.
4. Become genuinely interested in other people.
5. Make the other person feel important—and do it sincerely.
6. Show respect for the other man's opinions. Never tell a man he is wrong.
7. Begin in a friendly way.

8. Get the other person saying "yes, yes" immediately.
9. Let the other fellow feel that the idea is his.
10. Appeal to the nobler motives.
11. Call attention to people's mistakes indirectly.
12. Talk about your own mistakes before criticizing the other person.
13. Ask questions instead of giving direct orders.
14. Let the other man save his face.